BISON
BOOKS

Hull Cook, M.D.

Fifty Years a Country Doctor

University of Nebraska Press
Lincoln and London

⊗ The paper in this book meets

the minimum requirements of American

National Standard for Information

Sciences—Permanence of Paper

for Printed Library Materials,

ANSI Z39.48-1984.

Library of Congress

Cataloging-in-Publication Data

Cook, Hull, 1911–

Fifty years a country

doctor / Hull Cook.

p.   cm.

ISBN 0-8032-6389-9

(pbk. : alk. paper)

1. Cook, Hull, 1911–

2. Physicians (General practice)—

Nebraska—Biography.

3. Medicine, Rural—Nebraska.

I. Title.

RJ54.C564A3   1998

610′.92—dc21

[B]   97–50636

CIP

This book is gratefully dedicated to my long-suffering family and to the many trusting souls who put their lives in my hands.

Preface

This book presents something of a "Then and Now" recording of the practice of medicine over the past fifty years. The changes seem incredible. In addition, it gives a bit of insight into life as it was lived in rural Nebraska in the mid-portion of the twentieth century. Although limited in scope, the material herein presented is true. It is more personal than general. If in places it sounds somewhat bizarre, you must remember that times change.

One

The first day was a shocker. The first subject was anatomy. An attendant wheeled in a cadaver on a gurney and unceremoniously pulled off the covering sheet. The exposed body looked like a wet mummy, since it had just recently been fished out of the embalming tank.

The instructor arose and took charge. With poised scalpel he said, "Gentlemen, we will begin this demonstration with the dissection of the arm." And without waiting for us to adjust to the situation or the smell of the pickled unfortunate before us, he made a long, bold incision from one shoulder down across the pectoral region.

One student passed out. Another rushed from the room to throw up.

But we got used to it. We had to. This was medical school.

Anatomy was the course most feared by the students because it demanded that the memory retain a nearly encyclopedic knowledge of the human body, the infinite anatomical relationships between organs, bones, nerves, arteries, muscles, and other structures. We had to learn the position of each organ in relation to its surroundings: what was above and below it, to right and left of it, and before and behind it. One student was so frightened in an oral exam that he forgot momentarily the differentiation between male and female. In describing the relationship of the pelvic organs he averred that the prostate gland was in relation anterior to the uterus. The instructor admitted that while the statement might be true under certain circumstances, he could give no credit for this answer.

We were paired off, and each pair was given a cadaver to live with, to dissect, to study, and to revere as a silent teacher. Our cadaver was an elderly male of seventy or eighty years.

"What shall we call him?" queried my partner, Fagan White from Kansas.

As I drew off the rubberized sheet I noticed the diagnostic tag on his ankle. "Looks like his name was Arthur," I replied. "The tag says 'Art Sclerosis.'"

"OK. Art or Arthur, good enough."

"Wait a minute," I said. "Let's call him Ernest."

"What's the matter with Art? Why Ernest?"

"Because we'll be working in dead earnest."

I thought I was being especially clever; hence I was surprised at my partner's seemingly distressed hesitation at accepting the name. But he reluctantly agreed, and we diligently set to work "in dead earnest." Some weeks later I learned the name of my partner's older brother: Ernest.

During the months of dissection the student unwillingly carried with him the distinctive odor of his particular cadaver. It was in his hair, his clothes, his fingernails (we had no gloves), sometimes even on his breath. His outside acquaintances either turned away or asked what that awful smell was. Even students with enough money to date found their popularity waning. The student might order a nice dinner only to have his date suddenly say, "My appetite seems to have left me." The worst thing for the anatomy student was that he became so accustomed to the stench of his cadaver that he was unable to evaluate the degree of his offensiveness. We learned that if everyone moves away, you still stink.

Our schooling was taking place in an era of plentiful cadavers. A state law had been passed that gave all unidentified bodies to the medical school; thus there was a constantly renewable supply. They were embalmed and placed in a tank of preservative fluid containing phenol, formaldehyde, glycerine, and other chemicals that prevented hardening of the tissues. Their availability was of great advantage to scientific learning. Even the most squeamish opponents of dissection would, I'm sure, prefer that their surgeons have some such experience before slicing into their living tissues.

Before the era of plentiful cadavers, however, public opinion often condemned dissection of the human body. If you needed a body to study, you went out late at night with a shovel and a dim lantern to a secluded cemetery and dug one up. It is my understanding that the medical schools secretly condoned these midnight raids as a necessary evil.

We were told of two students who had thus procured a body one night. Even though the hour was late they feared detection when driving their wagon through town; so they had brought along a couple of blankets to cover and conceal the body, whom we'll call "Joe." After loading Joe into the wagon box and getting him comfortably covered, they were still worried. "What's it look like to you?" queried one.

"A dead body covered with blankets."

"Yeah. Let's drag him up onto the seat."

"What?!"

"We can set him up between us on the seat. Nobody can tell the difference."

"I can!"

"So what? Let's try it."

Accordingly, an average-looking spring wagon pulled by an average-looking team of horses proceeded inconspicuously through town. What if the seat appeared crowded? At that hour who would notice?

The boys' nerves were understandably jumpy, but their apparently undetected success was a heady experience. The situation called for a drink, and close by was a saloon with very few people in evidence. They halted. Tossing out the line weight, they left Joe slumped on the seat, apparently holding the horses, while they slipped inside for a stiff bracer.

Enter here onto the scene a third student who was aware of the

3

raid and was watching for the return of the wagon. He wanted to share in the excitement but feared to participate in the dig. Just in time, he checked his impulse to rush into the saloon. Instead he rolled Joe back into the wagon box and took Joe's place on the seat.

Ere long the two exuberant grave robbers returned, taking their places on either side of the supposed Joe. One took up the lines and clucked to the horses. The other turned to support Joe and check on his position. There was just enough light for him to see Joe turn and nod his head appreciatively. With a horrified croak the student leaped over the front wheel and disappeared. The driver, of course, whirled to see what was the matter, so Joe obligingly nodded to him also, thus shattering his composure and bravado. Like his companion he jumped from the wagon and started running, leaving the supposed friend, Joe's impostor, to drive on with the ill-gotten prize.

Two

"January!" I roared at my Number One burro as she stopped for a mouthful of mountain flowers. "Hike!"

Four pack burros and I were on the trail to Fern Lake, bringing supplies up to Fern Lodge, located at one of the most beautiful spots in Rocky Mountain National Park. The year was 1929. From the open porch at Fern there stretched forth a delightful panorama of mountains, forest, and deep blue lake. Notch Top Mountain and the Little Matterhorn dominated the view across the lake, with Mt. Gable and Stones Peaks reaching skyward a bit to the right. The fortunate observer was bathed in peace, beauty, and tranquillity at their best. Accommodations, though Spartan, were comfortable; the cuisine, superb.

Guests and employees were housed in log cabins scattered throughout the nearby woods. Running water was found only in the kitchen, piped in icy cold from a hillside spring. I'm using the past tense because the lodge has long since been dismantled and destroyed by the Park Service.

As packer my job was to bring in all supplies, baggage, and equipment necessary to operate this isolated wilderness hotel. There was, and still is, no road. The route was a rough horse trail that climbed fifteen hundred feet in five miles. Guests arrived on horseback or on foot. The packer was responsible for all their gear.

On the trail, trudging behind the burros, I had plenty of time to think. What was I really doing packing burros? My father kidded me good-naturedly for what he called my D.D. degree (Donkey Driver).

I thought back five years to when I was fourteen and working for a livery stable. The old blacksmith who kept our horses shod wanted me to join him as an apprentice. He promised to teach me how to shape horseshoes to improve the performance of gaited horses.

"We can follow the races, too, and shoe race horses. There's good money in that."

My father was not enthusiastic about the idea, but he issued no preventive ultimatum. He merely said: "Son, there's certainly nothing wrong with being a blacksmith or farrier. It's a perfectly honorable profession. Yet if you settle for that as your life's work you will realize somewhere down the road that you're not making full use of your talents, and you'll regret not having gone farther with your education."

He was right, of course. Even at fourteen I respected my father's opinions. He had a great track record for being right.

I already had one year as a geology major at the University of Colorado. Was that what I really wanted? For a teenager the selection of a life work is scary, exciting but scary. What if I should fail?

I planned to have a family, and I wanted my family to be able to speak with pride when referring to my occupation. Although any job well done deserves respect, an image of the family doctor kept coming to mind.

My interest in geology stemmed from my love of nature, the drama of orogeny, and the earth's history. Here was inexhaustible material for research and study. Yet I began to realize that I was more interested in people. And I needed to get into a line of work in which my inherent lazy streak would not hamper success. I should be working at something that would make people come to me and force me to get off my duff—make me get busy. I felt that I might need prodding. Boy, did I get prodded!

Along with geology, I had considered a career in medicine for a long time. It would be more personal. It would be me. I would not be working for some big corporation.

When I finally made the decision, it seemed to come almost abruptly. No more hesitation. I would be a doctor.

And so began the transition from D.D. to M.D.

My father was overjoyed. "Son," he exclaimed, "you could not have pleased me more. As you know, I wanted from early childhood to be a doctor. I never considered anything else."

Father had lacked the money to attend medical school. At that time dental school was less expensive, so he had reluctantly settled for that. He became a dentist, and a good one. Now he was reliving his ambition in me.

"Do you have the vision?" he asked.

"The vision?" I replied lamely.

"Yes, the vision. All through my youth I had the vision. I imagined being able to walk in and relieve pain and suffering. I wanted to help people—to be needed. Do you feel that way?

I agreed, not wishing to dampen his euphoria, although a few years elapsed before I began really to feel deeply what he had felt since childhood. It seemed bonded to humility, and it came actually as a gift from my patients. Now it was back to college, the University of Colorado, for the additional two years of premedic credits.

"What do you mean, for Heaven's sake? My high school diploma!" My frustration was rapidly becoming anger. Here I was seeking admission to the medical school class of 1936 with all my credentials approved, and this dean's office clerk was demanding to see my high school diploma.

"I don't have it," I said flatly. "It wouldn't fit into my records box, so I cut out the seal and threw the rest away. You have all my premed records from this same university. That should be all that's needed. I would not have been admitted for premed without proof of high school graduation."

"I can't accept that excuse," said Miss Rule Book stiffly. "If you have no diploma I cannot process your admission until we have an affidavit from your high school certifying to the fact that you have graduated."

It's not my nature to be meek. When confronted with a difficult situation, I am more inclined to take forceful action, to follow the advice of a "crazy" uncle who said, "You should just grab the bull by the tail and look the situation in the face." Because there's nothing lower than a freshman, however, I stifled my anger at Miss Rule Book and sought out my high school principal.

"So you made it into medical school!" he exclaimed with a hint of unflattering surprise.

The affidavit was no problem, and soon I was starting medical school, resolved to study like mad so that no one would die as a result of my failure to learn.

Three

I should like to say something of my family, since they have added so much meaning to my life, and without them I would have been something of a hollow shell. I was married in 1939 to Ruth Joy Muirhead, a cute, intelligent girl whose father some years earlier had been dean of Creighton Medical School in Omaha. She had come to Sidney in midterm to fill a vacancy left by a teacher who had quit her job to be married. As a graduate dietitian Ruth was awaiting the start of her dietetic internship in a hospital in Seattle. She began taking her evening meals at Mrs. Roger's boardinghouse, where I lived.

It took me six months to get her to the altar. Our wedding took place in Jackson Hole, Wyoming, in the little mission church at Moose. A few years earlier, while riding in search of stray horses, I had come upon this isolated little church. Intrigued by its beautiful setting in view of the Tetons, I went inside. The solitude and the awesome setting affected me deeply. I resolved that when I got married, the ceremony would occur here. And here we were.

There is some question as to the legality of our wedding. Two witnesses were required. We had only one, a parishioner who was cleaning the church. But she had her two small children with her who stood in with us, and two children should equal one adult.

After the ceremony Ruth carefully pressed our wedding certificate in a magazine to protect it. The magazine got thrown away. No proof.

But we launched on our honeymoon anyway, a week in the wilderness with two saddle horses and two packhorses obtained from Scotty at Brooks Lake. For one who had never camped out, Ruth adapted amazingly well. Our week in the solitude of the mountains was fantastic.

After our privileged stay in this primitive paradise, I brought Ruth back to Sidney. We built a modest home, and as the years sped by we were blessed, really blessed because they are such a delight, with three children: Susan, Sandra, and a boy, Hull, whom I playfully called "Cactus," a nickname that has stuck to him ever since.

At age four Susan was remarkably perceptive in evaluating the life of a country doctor. "Out of the mouths of babes," one might say. When asked whether she planned to become a doctor when she grew up, she replied soberly, "I don't know. You have to work like a dog to be a doctor!" Perhaps she had overheard Ruth's somewhat forlorn comment when I flopped wearily on the couch one day: "Your public gets all the goody out of you."

Another time Susan said to her mother, "Mommy, let's have a party."

"All right," answered her mother. "What's the occasion?"

"Daddy's home!"

Without such a loving, understanding family, a doctor's life could be a disaster. In return for the unquestioning support I received from my entire family I endeavored to make life as interesting for them as time would permit. We took short vacation trips as a family, usually in the mountains of Colorado, Wyoming, and New Mexico. We even tried ranching, first in Wyoming, then in Montana. With a competent ranch family on the property the year-round, we could be absentee ranchers and come and go as time permitted. Although we made occasional visits throughout the year, August always found us there, enjoying a fun-filled month of work and play that was both educational and satisfying. The kids loved it.

Four

During the first months of the freshman year I lived at a fraternity house, a situation that sounded like a good idea. The upperclassmen could be very helpful at times, although they were often too busy. One incident impressed me with the practicality of fraternal cooperation. A senior had picked up a girl somewhere and had taken her up to his room. Somehow under the guise of foreplay he had secretly taken a vaginal smear on a microscope slide. This is smuggled to a fraternity brother, who rushed to his microscope. A report of "no gonorrhea germs seen" was relayed upstairs in time for the prolonged foreplay to give way to more serious action. I was awed. These seniors knew everything!

Despite such interesting episodes, life at the frat house began losing its appeal because of frequent noisy disturbances that rendered study difficult. Because I worked at the hospital cafeteria for my meals, my limited study time required efficient utilization.

My dissection partner had rented a basement room near the school for ten dollars a month. The rent was cheap even for those days because the landlord, whose job as a railway mail clerk required that he be away much of the time, wanted a man in the house at night to protect his wife and small daughter. It developed that I would be permitted to share the room with no increase in rent. Possibly I was to protect the wife from renter Number One, a line of thinking that could lead to a progression. At any rate, five dollars a month was a figure I could afford.

Our landlord was Lloyd Paste (and wife, Hazel), whose real names I use because they were such fine people. When we moved in they said, "Now, boys, we want you to feel at home. Any time you need a snack just raid the refrigerator. If it's at night and you don't find what you want and we're in bed, just knock on our door. We'll be glad to get up and get you something!"

I couldn't believe it. Of course, with each of us paying five dollars a month rent I suppose we could expect fringe benefits. Needless to say, we never routed them out of bed. In fact, it was rare indeed for us even to peek in their refrigerator. I recall one night, however, when Scorp, my roommate, did fix a small snack.

"We really shouldn't do this," I admonished.

"Oh, they won't mind," he replied with a chuckle, then added with an amusing inversion of logic, "They can deduct it from our room rent."

Since working at the cafeteria was taking valuable time which I felt should be applied to study, I considered "batching" in our basement room. When the landlord heard of this, he offered to provide me with a small gas stove and a cupboard. He had already installed a shower near our room. With the little stove I was all set. At a neighborhood grocery I was able to buy wilted vegetables to make soup. These were cheaper and still OK when cooked. Sometimes the grocer gave me the wilts and rejects free. A big pot of soup would last several days. My food bill was under ten dollars a month.

It is not accurate, however, to maintain that I was subsisting on batching alone. Often on weekends I would be "eating up a storm" at the home of Bob and Dorothy Collier, where, oddly enough, I seemed always welcome, probably because during the summers I was in their employ as a guide on Longs Peak.

The attrition rate among our freshman class was frightening. Every few days or weeks someone would flunk out. After the full four years we were a graduating class of fifty. We had started out with ninety freshmen and had picked up ten transfers, which meant that fifty of the original ninety had flunked out, 55 percent. The specter of failure was ever-present.

I attribute my diploma not to intelligence but to being too stubborn to give up. Besides, my parents were counting on me. I simply could not let them down, although they never pressured me, bless them. Their support was both emotional and financial. The only time Father ever offered direct criticism was in response to a depressing letter I had written the year after I had received my diploma. During my first month as a surgical intern, I followed a friend who had often assisted his father in surgery. He could handle instruments and tie knots in a way that made me look as if I were all thumbs. In a discouraged mood I wrote home stating that I was evidently not "surgeon material." Back came a letter by return mail in which Father said, "Get that crazy idea out of your head. Just get in there and do it."

At school there were occasional amusing breaks in the crushing schedule. In biochemistry class we endured a project that required the chemical analysis of a twenty-four-hour urine specimen. This called for saving all voidings over a twenty-four-hour period. We were each given a transparent gallon jug and the challenge to fill it. Whether we were in the halls or on the street or riding the bus to and from school, we were thus saddled with the foamy evidence of our output. Some of the more timid concealed their jugs in paper bags, and one embarrassed student sought to confuse bystanders with a large label that read "BEER," but his generous offers of free drinks to classmates were rejected.

In physiology class it seemed we were always operating on dogs and recording the effects of various medications on heart rate, blood pressure, respiration, and the like. The dogs were, of course, anesthetized and often overdosed with anesthetic so they would die humanely instead of having to attempt a nearly hopeless recovery. But if the dog should die before all experiments were completed and duly recorded, the whole project would have to be repeated on another dog, perhaps a three- or four-hour job.

One day our team was near enough to completing our experiments that we felt that if the dog died we could fake the rest. We would soon find out because just then the dog expired. Soon after, we were dismayed to see the head professor approaching on his rounds of inspection. He cast a baleful eye on our table. "Your dog's dead," he announced accusingly.

"Oh, no. I believe he's still going," I replied with as much conviction as I could muster for such a fib. To prove his point, the professor clapped his stethoscope on the dog's chest. I was standing on the opposite side and was able surreptitiously to tap a fake heartbeat with my finger. The professor looked puzzled.

"The sounds are pretty weak. He's about gone. You'd better hurry." Thank goodness he passed on to the next table without noticing that our dog's respirations were shallow to the point of being nonexistent.

In an internal medicine class an eccentric professor wheeled in a machine nearly as large as a piano. It had wires on it that he connected to a sick patient as if to electrocute him. Then he rigged an apparatus to record the patient's heartbeat. It was novel but obviously of little use since you could easily listen to anyone's heart with a stethoscope. He called the contraption an electrocardiograph. We were looking at the precursor of today's elaborate electronic heart monitors. Times change!

In a discussion of oxygen assimilation, our physiology professor mentioned that oxygen could not be stored in the body for more than a minute or two, a statement that stirred doubts in my mind, which I had the temerity to express. I said, "I believe that if I can breathe pure oxygen for two minutes I can hold my breath for several minutes."

The professor was very tolerant and sufficiently curious to let me try. An oxygen tank was brought in, and I was permitted to breathe pure oxygen for two minutes.

"It will burn your lungs," warned a classmate. But I felt no discomfort as I took deep breaths of the pure stuff. I was lying on a lab table, where I could remain motionless to minimize oxygen consumption.

The timing began. I had a clamp on my nose, and my mouth was taped shut. After three minutes my classmates began to show increased interest. Pearl divers are able to remain submerged much longer than this despite their vigorous exertion, so my three minutes at complete rest was nothing remarkable. And I had another advantage: I had recently been living at an altitude of nearly thirteen thousand feet, which had increased my red blood cell count to over six million.

Four minutes went by—and five. Bystanders were asking, "Is he still going?" "Blink your eyes if you're OK."

I was beginning to feel a strong urge to breathe, probably as much from the need to expel carbon dioxide as from oxygen depletion.

At eight minutes I could no longer ignore the heaving of my diaphragm. I had to rip off the tape and gasp hungrily for air. I had proved only that oxygen could be stored for several minutes if the body were first saturated with it. I confess that the experiment was partly an expression of an imaginary macho image. I enjoyed attempting things that were considered impossible.

Sixty years later I related the incident to Dr. "Brownie" Schoene, a well-known pulmonary specialist in Seattle and an authority on high-altitude respiration. I expected him to doubt the story. To my surprise, he replied enthusiastically, "I tried the same experiment." Naturally I wondered how close he had come to my record. Over a friendly grin he added, "I managed thirteen minutes."

So much for my macho image. Then he really punctured my ego by adding, "The record is fifteen minutes! At least that's the highest I've heard of. It's held by Dr. Herman Rahn, a pulmonary physiologist at Buffalo, New York. He's now deceased." No wonder, I thought, remembering how I felt at eight minutes.

One of our classmates was dubbed the "Fire Chief," a title he acquired through an unusual incident. A nationally famous fan dancer was performing in town. All of the boys who could afford a ticket were planning to go. Those of us who could not were somewhat dejected. The subsequent "Fire Chief" reassured us, "Don't feel bad, boys. After the performance I'll bring her around so you can all meet her."

"Yeah, yeah. Sure. Naturally. Do that. You move that fast and we'll call you the 'Fire Chief.'"

Try to imagine our utter amazement and delight when our fast-moving brother appeared about 11:30 that evening with Sally on his arm. This was no minor coup. I said she was nationally famous, probably internationally would be more accurate. We were dazzled! We couldn't believe it! From that day on our respect, and envy, for Chief's prowess with the ladies knew no bounds.

He did let me in on a secret, something I have not divulged until now: he and Sally had grown up together as neighbors. "I was fairly sure," he added, "that she would be pleased to see me." His nickname was "Chief" for the rest of his life.

Five

As yet our work was not all with live patients. I recall an amusing and painful incident in obstetrics class. A delivery table was wheeled into the amphitheater with a "pregnant" mannequin on it. Our British-sounding professor surveyed the assembled students with haughty disdain and called for volunteers to demonstrate the use of forceps. None of the usual "smart-ass" group volunteered, so he selected two victims and asked that they come forward.

"You have studied the use of the obstetrical forceps. We will now have a demonstration of their application. You," indicating one, "will apply the forceps. And you," the other, "will provide the labor contractions."

The forceps is the tonglike instrument that enables the operator to pull on the baby and thus facilitate its passage through the birth canal. In addition to having a cephalic curve to fit the infant's head, it also has a pelvic curve like rocking chair rockers to fit the posterior curve of the mother's pelvis.

The forceps rattled audibly in the hands of the terrified accoucheur, not from stage fright but because he was in the lower half of the class scholastically and hence was in constant fear of being weeded out. He must demonstrate at least a modicum of capability. He separated the two blades of the forceps as must be done before insertion is attempted. He laid one aside. So far so good. In challenging mother and babe with the first blade, however, he managed to wiggle it in upside down. This, of course, made application of the matching blade incorrect also.

The mannequin was a life-sized female body made of rubberized material and having an open birth canal and a large slot in the abdomen into which could be inserted a rubber infant. In this case the baby was crammed rather tightly down into the pelvis where the apprentice accoucheur had the opportunity to apply the forceps to its head and thus facilitate delivery. While firm traction was being applied with the forceps, the assisting student was to press downward on the mannequin's abdomen to simulate labor contractions.

It should be mentioned here that there are several wrong ways to apply the forceps, some of which may cause injury to the infant and one, at least, to the mother. The latter involves putting the forceps in upside down so that the curved ends may dig backward and tear into the mother's rectum. I've never seen this happen in practice, but in our demonstration, with the student frightened half to death lest he flunk the course, it happened.

The professor's commentary on the proper procedure stopped abruptly when he observed this grievous mistake. No one spoke as our terrified amateur pulled on the forceps. Nothing moved. He pulled harder. His assistant, thinking to be of help, suddenly pressed vigorously on the abdomen. His maneuver was effective. The baby popped out unexpectedly like a projectile, struck the operator in the belly, and fell to the floor.

The professor could stand no more. He was livid. With nose in the air, he rocked back and forth on his heels and exploded. "Capital! Capital! Now you have but to strike the 'fathah' over the head with the forceps and you will have murdered the whole bloody family!"

Our accoucheur slunk back to his seat in disgrace. His assistant felt almost as bad, realizing that he had been a part of the disaster. One might have expected derisive laughter from the class, but there was silence. Each one was thinking, "There but for the grace of God go I." In fact, in recounting this episode I still feel a slight wave of anxiety.

On a happier note, I might add that both of the students involved received passing final grades. The professor's highly critical intolerance probably gave way to mirth after he had left the amphitheater. Nearly all of our professors, especially in the clinical studies, were practicing physicians who accepted part-time teaching positions at the medical school without pay. It was an honor accorded only to those who were highly respected in their fields. They kept us students scared so we would study. Actually most were very kind and understanding. They just pretended to be mean. Many were inspiring teachers. A long list of names would be boring, but I should like to mention Dr. Barber, pediatrician, for his informative oratory on infectious diseases; Dr. Ed Mugrage in clinical pathology for his understanding patience; and Dr. Cuthbert Powell for his dramatic presentation of obstetrics and gynecology. Also, Dr. Black in pathology was as fine a teacher as anyone could hope to meet. All of our old instructors have passed through the Pearly Gates. Pax.

It was in the junior year that we were endeavoring to develop proficiency in obstetrics. We were at last having daily contact with live patients. In obstetrics we were doing home deliveries with the assistance of a very competent registered nurse, someone who was a member of the Visiting Nurses' Association (VNA).

Our home deliveries took place in the poorer sections of Denver, and the patients, for the most part, were very appreciative of our efforts. The system had been worked out by the school and the VNA. A visiting nurse would respond quickly to the call of a woman in labor who had been seen previously in the clinic. The nurse would try to determine the stage of labor. When she felt that the doctor might soon be needed, she notified the school, which called one of the students on OB service and dispatched him to the scene, usually accompanied by an intern from the University Hospital. If any dangerous complications arose, the patient could be quickly transferred by ambulance to the hospital.

As students we were instructed to try to determine the degree of cervical dilatation by inserting a gloved finger in the woman's rectum and palpating the cervix through the thin rectal wall. This rectal exam was recommended to minimize the chance of introducing infection into the birth canal. It also often had the effect of dropping the patient's confidence in her new young doctor to zero. "What kind of idiot is this?" she would think. "He doesn't even know which passage the baby comes out of!" Reassurance was often difficult, especially if the patient did not speak English. I recall one woman crying out in great disgust, "Wrong hole! Wrong hole!"

If delivery seemed imminent, the patient would be placed crosswise on the bed with newspapers under her and a rubber Kelly pad under the buttocks with its "tongue" draped over the edge of the bed into a washtub or slop bucket. Each foot was placed on a chair on either side of the doctor, and the woman's hips were drawn to the edge of the bed. The doctor drew on sterile gloves, and, after the nurse flushed the vulva with antiseptic solution, he placed sterile drapes over the thighs and abdomen and under the buttocks.

Often at this point we were in for quite a wait. What appeared to be a vigorous labor often subsided for a time when our arrival relieved some of the patient's anxiety and enabled her to relax. Sometimes a few hours might go by while we waited, sitting or perhaps standing around, trying not to touch anything with our sterile gloves.

I recall one night asking the visiting nurse to pull up my pant leg quickly and kill the bedbug that had just "topped" my sock and was climbing higher. She kindly obliged, much to my relief. Our ultraclean landlady would have been distressed had I introduced bedbugs into her house.

As labor progressed, the intern would give drop ether on a mask whenever it seemed indicated. Most of the deliveries were relatively simple since these women had all been screened at the clinic for probable safe home delivery.

The fact that most women can be delivered safely at home has given rise to a popular "natural" cult consisting of an increasing number of proud (and lucky) fathers who have been their wife's only attendant at birth. Having experienced the joy of an easy natural childbirth and being ignorant of the many possible complications, they noisily acclaim the advantages of home over hospital. Those who follow their recommendations may find themselves confronted by a transverse presentation, a breech, an arm presentation, a series of terrifying convulsions, a dangerous hemorrhage, or a limp baby that refuses to breathe. And not all of these complications will wait for the arrival of outside assistance.

Fortunately, most of our home deliveries went fairly smoothly. Occasionally the woman would get a bit hysterical. Pain of childbirth can be severe, and our modest whiffs of ether were sometimes inadequate to alleviate it. I recall one high-strung young woman who kept screaming, "God, Jesus, Doctor! God, Jesus, Doctor!"

The visiting nurse nudged my elbow and commented, "You're moving in pretty fast company, aren't you, Doctor?"

We had available to us perhaps 2 percent of the diagnostic tests that are available today. This paucity of laboratory aids was not all bad. It forced us to obtain a careful history and to hone our senses of sight, sound, smell, and touch to a high degree of sensitivity.

The stethoscope figured prominently in diagnosis. In evaluating the heart and lungs, however, one could sometimes do almost as well by placing an ear directly to the chest. This reminds me of an incident the truth of which I'll not try to defend.

A very tired country doctor, upon arriving at the patient's home, discovered that he was without his stethoscope. He was far enough out in the country that a trip back to town was impractical. He would have to evaluate the woman's chest by direct auscultation.

"Madam, in my haste to respond to your call I seem to have come off without my stethoscope. I will need to place my ear on your chest to evaluate your heart and lungs."

Obligingly, she exposed her chest so that while sitting close to the bed he could lay his head on her breast.

"The heart sounds fine. Now I shall need to have you count for me to evaluate the resonance of the lungs. Please count, if you will, one, two, three, and so on."

The woman's ample bosom made a soft and comfortable pillow. The doctor did not realize the degree of his fatigue until he was suddenly started to hear the patient dutifully speaking, "327, 328, 329—!"

We proudly considered our surgery to be highly developed. Operations were even being done on the brain. Of course, such things as repairing or replacing valves in a living heart were brushed aside as preposterous.

Until 1936 we had no sulfa drugs, no penicillin, no antibiotics. We did have aspirin, digitalis, quinine, laxatives, and even insulin, plus a whole pharmacopoeia full of medicines, most of which were of questionable effectiveness. Nevertheless, we were required to memorize the dosages of a great many. Our only advantage was that few of them had any hazardous interactions. With today's specific and highly effective drugs we must be constantly aware of possible interactions, some of which are dangerous.

We doctors can claim very little credit for the tremendous advances in medications. It is the researchers who deserve the plaudits. Their job involves monotonous repetition and exacting evaluation. Imagine poor Dr. Erlich testing 605 substances and formulas before discovering one that was effective against syphilis. This one, No. 606, he called "arsphenamine," or "salvarsan." It contained arsenic and was widely used throughout the world against this miserable affliction.

The English referred to syphilis as the "French disease." The French blamed the Italians. The Italians called it the "Spanish disease." The Spanish claimed it was a gift from the Moors. I don't know who the Moors blamed. I suppose they had to kick the dog.

Salvarsan, besides causing an occasional allergic reaction, had three disadvantages:

It had to be given intravenously in 300 cc of fluid.

It was slow in effect, necessitating injections twice weekly for months or years.

If a bit of the solution were spilled in the tissue surrounding the vein, an angry slough (destroying) of local tissue was apt to occur.

Erlich and others continued their search for something better, eventually reaching test compound No. 914. It was a related arsenical, which Erlich called neo-arsphenamine. It could be given in a 10 cc syringe, thus eliminating the need for having the patient lying down for thirty or forty minutes. I've often wondered whether the number of the salvarsan inspired the name of the old 606 nightclub in Chicago.

Researchers discovered that bismuth was also a partially effective agent so the two were often used in conjunction: eight weeks of arsenic alternating with eight weeks of bismuth. This schedule had the advantage of resting the veins and kidneys while on bismuth (which was given intramuscularly in the buttocks) and resting the derriere while on arsenic. The treatment was continued for a minimum of two years, a far cry from today's brief round of high-dose penicillin.

In later years many a former case of syphilis was unexpectedly identified by an x-ray of the pelvis when small bits of long-unabsorbed bismuth in the buttocks were made visible on the film. These residual bits are seldom seen today. They're a bit too far in the past.

Mercury rubs also were helpful in discouraging the germ (spirochete) of syphilis. A single dose of mercury ointment was wrapped in wax paper by the pharmacist. This amount was to be rubbed well into the skin three times weekly, using a different area of the body each time until, running out of areas, the patient went back to square one and followed through again. Mercury was favored in patients showing sensitivity to arsenic. It must have been hard on the liver and kidneys. Furthermore, it took longer than arsenic, giving rise to the ominous slogan, "Five minutes with Venus and five years with Mercury," a wisecrack that was amusing only to those who had never had syphilis.

A senior intern in Denver certainly was not amused. In withdrawing a needle from a patient with active syphilis he accidentally pricked his finger. One would usually expect to escape unharmed. Not so here. A primary chancre developed at the site of the needle puncture. (A chancre is the dime-sized punched-out ulcer of the skin that appears at the site where the spirochete drilled its way into the body. It is the first sign that a person has become infected, and it appears only once.)

"And to think," he complained, "I didn't even have any fun catching it!" Nonetheless, he was condemned to the usual two years of intensive treatment.

The Wassermann blood test was being used then to diagnose syphilis. A positive reaction would be reported at 1+ to 4+, depending on the degree of reaction. In general, a 4+ reaction was taken to indicate an active case. A 1+ was more apt to be an old case, perhaps a treated one. One of the staff doctors was so unpopular that the students referred to him as "the guy whose Wassermann is higher than his IQ."

A patient might admit to having had a "slight touch" of the disease, yet syphilis is syphilis, and such an admission is comparable to a girl's being just a wee bit pregnant. A more definitive test than the Wassermann is the dark field microscopic examination, in which the spirochetes can be observed directly, spiraling their way about the field, looking for a place where they can bore in.

During the sixties there was a popular TV program entitled *Have Gun; Will Travel*. It featured an old-time western gunman who was available for hire. He was called Paladin. One of the many possible lesions caused by the treponema pallidum (the syphilis spirochete) is a gumma, a type of abscess. At a medical convention in a booth presenting the latest in the treatment of syphilis, a clever salesman displayed a large placard that read, "Treponema Pallidum. Have Gumma; Will Travel."

We had no way of determining with certainty when a syphilitic patient could be pronounced cured. If the Wassermann became negative, we hoped that cure had been effected. If it remained positive after two years of treatment, we were inclined to give an additional two months of the dreaded shots before assuring the patient that he was apparently cured. The only real proof of cure occurred occasionally when one of our subjects returned with a brand new chancre. Ta-da!!!

Six

During the last half of our junior year Jim Donnelly and I obtained junior internships at one of the Denver hospitals. Officially there was no such position as junior intern, but the hospital needed more semiprofessional help, so we were given that status. It was a part-time, flunky job, mostly doing histories and physicals to supply information for patients' charts. We also did emergency lab work at night, and started IVs when the regular interns were busy or off duty.

Late one night an elderly doctor from a rural community in eastern Colorado brought in a very sick diabetic child with measles. Rash, high fever, and unconsciousness were obvious. The boy, age six, had been getting by on a rather strict diet until the measles struck. As the fever mounted, he became unconscious. The doctor reasoned correctly that he needed insulin. Being unfamiliar with insulin dosage, he had administered only five units and, a bit later, another five. The boy was getting worse so the doctor recommended hospitalization because he hated for the boy to die at home.

As it happened, Jim and I were spending the night at the hospital, studying between interruptions for an exam the next day on internal medicine. Diabetes figured prominently in our studies. The boy's doctor explained that he had given the ten units and now did not know whether the problem was insulin shock or diabetic coma.

Jim and I had no doubts. The boy had stertorous breathing, and you could smell acetone the minute you walked into the room. Jim palpated his eyeballs for slight mushiness, and we both spoke up almost at once, "The kid's in diabetic coma."

"You're sure?"

"Yes, indeed. He's in diabetic acidosis due to high blood sugar. He needs IV fluids and a lot more insulin. The measles has greatly increased his insulin requirement."

"Well, you boys seem to understand the situation better than I. Will you be on duty all night?"

"Yes, all night."

"In that case I'll turn him over to you and go get a hotel room. You write the orders. I'll be at the Cosmopolitan. Call me when he dies."

Can you imagine a scenario like that in a reputable hospital of today? We were juniors in medical school, two years below the level of intern, and writing orders like qualified M.D.s. But things were less restrictive back in the thirties.

Jim and I started an IV at once. We had no way of determining the boy's blood sugar level, but we knew it had to be sky high. We were not many years beyond the time when, to diagnose diabetes, the doctor had to taste the urine—yes, taste it for sweetness—or spill a little on the floor and step in it to see whether it seemed sticky.

Of course, no one had ever heard of insulin receptors, those built-in regulators that limit the amount of insulin the body can utilize. We did know that if we did not correct his diabetic acidosis within the next few hours he would die.

We gave him forty units under the skin, forty units in the IV of lactated Ringer's, and another forty along toward morning.

At 7:30 his doctor phoned. "I haven't heard from you boys. Is our patient still alive?"

"Yes, he is!" we replied cheerfully.

"How do you think he is doing?"

"Well, right now he's sitting up on the edge of the bed wolfing down his breakfast."

"Good Lord! Is that possible? How much insulin has he had?

"We have given him 120 units."

"My God! I'll be right out. Thank you so much!"

Our joyful exuberance over the successful outcome completely overshadowed our fatigue. While guarding the boy's condition, we had quizzed each other all night in preparation for the examination. We both did well on it, and we felt no fatigue until it was completed. Then we collapsed.

The warm glow of achievement derived from actually saving this child's life was a great soporific. (And it spawned a realization of some of the vision Father had described.)

Since the junior internship provided only board, room, and experience, money was always in short supply, yet the search for a job that could be fitted into my schedule seemed futile. It certainly never occurred to me to inquire in a dance hall. Several years had passed since I had played trumpet, and I had not the time to be a janitor. A surprise was coming.

On a Saturday night I was making my first visit to a downtown dance hall. I was pleased to find the regular dancing interrupted at mid-evening for a few sets of old-time square dancing. Having received some recognition previously as a square-dance caller, I felt a kindred spirit with the man who was calling these sets. I approached him at intermission for a bit of camaraderie.

He regarded me with interest. Since the revival of square dancing was just getting under way, callers were scarce. "You mean you can call?" he asked, excitedly, I thought.

I confessed that I could.

"Well, come with me. Let's talk to the boss. I need a vacation."

He led me to a small office where sat a dour-looking man who scarcely noticed our entrance. "I've found a replacement," announced my new friend enthusiastically. "Now I can take my vacation."

The boss was not impressed. Few callers were as youthful as I. He sniffed. "What makes you think he can call? Have you heard him?"

"Not exactly. But I know he's good. I've talked to him."

Such favorable billing after just a two-minute conversation amazed me. "Let him prove it," commented the boss indifferently. "Have him call the next sets."

I was about to have a job thrust unexpectedly upon me, a once-a-week job that paid five dollars for only thirty minutes of what to me was recreation. I was amazed and delighted. Handing me the mike, the caller suggested, "Call anything you like, but not too complicated at first." Sets were already squared and eager for action. I signaled the band.

"Saloo-oot your company and the lady on your left," I sang into the mike in the rhythmic jargon of the "called" quadrille and proceeded to run through two sets, after which the regular caller grabbed me again for a second interview with the boss. Gratifying applause followed us as we again entered the small office. "OK," remarked the boss, "Take your vacation." And to me, "Be here at nine o'clock next Saturday."

The regular caller must have found something he liked better, for he did not return, thus leaving me the job for the remainder of the school year.

I had learned square dancing (and calling) while teaching school at Pinon, Colorado, in the years 1929–30. Its various forms fascinated me. I was hooked.

During the next several years I organized a few small dance groups and had heaps of fun dancing and especially calling, an art that I spent many hours trying to perfect. About 1935 some friends encouraged me to enter the Colorado State Square Dance Callers contest in Colorado Springs, where, to my astonishment, I was awarded second place. I was amused at a comment one of the judges made to me afterward. He said, "If you were older, and had a little manure on your boots, we'd have given you First."

Seven

Miraculously, our senior year arrived, and with it came a comfortable feeling of accomplishment that permitted some degree of relaxation. We were going to make it after all.

During this senior year I wangled a junior internship at another Denver hospital. Frequently I would cover for one or more of the regular interns, a practice that could be scary and was probably illegal had anyone bothered to find out.

A call suddenly advised me that I was needed in surgery. Why me, I thought, rushing to answer the summons. I'm no surgeon. Then I remembered that the two interns who were supposed to be on call had signed out to me. I grabbed cap and mask and entered the surgical suite. The surgeon regarded me skeptically. We had never seen each other before. "This lady needs a cut-down quickly. We can't find her veins."

The circulating nurse folded back the sterile drapes, exposing the patient's legs to the knees. When the patient is lying down and on the verge of shock, the veins practically disappear. I donned the sterile gloves proffered by the nurse, somehow finding the appropriate openings for all fingers, a feat not always easy for an amateur. Having identified what I hoped was a vein, I began diligently scrubbing the area with antiseptic.

"Hurry it up if you can," snapped the surgeon testily. "She needs that blood."

This was to be my first cut into a living person, a very minor procedure to be sure, but I still had to pick up a knife and cut. I prayed that I might find a vein, any vein, and that I could insert the cannula (tube) in time to restore the patient's blood pressure.

"We haven't got all day!" exploded the surgeon. "Is that blood running yet?"

At that moment I was able to express a relieved, "Yes, Sir."

As the cannula was secured with a ligature and the job completed, I felt a wave of profound gratitude to the dogs that had been sacrificed so that I might learn this simple procedure before having to perform it quickly on a human being.

The circulating nurse happened to be the wife of the intern who was "scrubbed in" assisting the surgeon. She realized my inexperience and my anxiety, and we both knew I was not supposed to be doing what I had just done. I appreciated deeply her reassurance when she touched me and whispered most kindly, "Had my husband done that well I would be very proud of him." Nurses are mostly a wonderful lot.

Graduation at last seemed inevitable. From a distant questionable mirage, it was assuming tangible reality. Graduation exercises, however, are about as entertaining as watching a mule switch his tail at flies. Consequently, not long before the appointed day I let it be known at home that I preferred not to attend. My diploma would be sent to me by mail if I so desired.

I have never seen my mother come unglued. She has always been a very calm person and still is at the age of 104. But when she heard my intentions, her boiler pressure shot up to the red line, and she exclaimed incredulously, "What did you say?"

I said, "I see no need to attend the actual ceremony."

At this my mother fixed a steely eye upon me and stated with almost ferocious intensity: "Your father and I are going to attend. And *you* had better be there!"

I was there.

Eight

For my internship, the Robert B. Greene Memorial Hospital and I chose each other. It was through an unusual coincidence that I even heard of the Greene. It was not on our list of hospitals. In visiting with a man who sold medical books I learned that he had many years ago attended normal school with my mother in Kansas. He took an interest in my search for a good internship, mentioning especially the Robert B. Greene Hospital of San Antonio, Texas, saying: "If you go to one of those big fancy hospitals you'll not even get close to a patient in surgery. The first assistant and the second assistant will both have to drop dead before you can get close enough to get a hand in the wound. All you'll get to do is watch. At the Greene you'll *be* the surgeon." How right he was!

There were twelve of us interns. We were to rotate duty through all the services, spending one or two months on each: surgery, medicine, orthopedics, obstetrics, pediatrics, and so on. Dr. J. B. Copeland was administrator at the time. After our orientation meeting, he singled me out. "Dr. Cook, we've had only one man from Colorado before you, Dr. Gatewood C. Milligan, and he was so damn good that the board wanted to try another man from Colorado. You've got something to live up to."

I was already apprehensive as to how I would stack up against the other interns, most of whom were from larger eastern schools, perhaps selected because of the prestigious reputation of those schools. Although Dr. Copeland's admonishment was intended merely as an incentive for me to do my best, it seemed to hang over my head like an ominous warning.

As interns we were there to serve and to learn. We were not pampered. In addition to our room, board, laundry, and all the aspirin we could eat, we received a salary. It was not a big salary. It was ten dollars a month. Plainly an intern would not acquire great wealth at the Greene. And yet I did acquire great wealth, not in dollars but in knowledge through up-front experience with some of the worst cases in every field. I remember thinking many times, "No matter what they bring to me in private practice, I will be prepared by having seen something worse at the Greene."

The Greene at that time was the city and county hospital of San Antonio and Bexar County, Texas (pronounced "bay-har" but sounds more like "bear" in conversation). We referred to it as the "Duele House" ("duele" meaning pain in Spanish), or simply as the "Bucket of Blood."

We were truly responsible for the patients on our service. Certain practicing physicians in town took turns being chief of the service that was their specialty. They would try to make rounds daily to supervise what we interns were doing to or for the patients, but most of the decisions were ours.

For example, we might call the chief of surgery and say, "We've got a man with stab wounds of the belly. We've notified OR. Do you want to come out?"

The chief would probably ask, "Do you think you can handle it?"

"I think so."

"All right. Get one of the boys to help you. Call me if you get into trouble." Surprisingly, most of the patients did well.

I was aghast at having so much responsibility thrust upon me from the very first day. On that day Dr. Crouch, the retiring surgical intern, made rounds with me so I could take over all of his patients on the surgical wards. "My God!" I thought. "I'm really expected to assume care of these people. They are really sick. They need a doctor. Good Heavens! I am their doctor."

Dr. Crouch stopped at the bedside of a very sick-looking man.

"This fellow," he said, "had a badly ruptured liver. Bled like hell. We had to pack his liver with surgical lap packs. That was two days ago." Then he advised, "I wouldn't try to pull the packs for a few days, unless you want to clean blood off the ceiling."

Again I was appalled at the seriousness of the job I was expected to assume. Surgery was to be my first assignment. I prayed that I could supply what these people needed, these people with the staring, questioning eyes. They knew that I was new to the job, and they wondered.

Nearly two-thirds of the patients were Mexican, about one-fourth were black, and the remaining few were Anglos. Many of the Mexicans spoke no English. A relative or a hospital employee often volunteered as an interpreter, but I could sense that what I got from them lacked the zest and color of the original. I found that I could do better dealing directly with the patients. When they found that I was trying to learn their language, they outdid themselves with various mimelike antics, some hysterical, to help me understand.

My education in Spanish was fostered by an elderly Mexican man on the orthopedic ward who assumed the responsibility of teaching me a new word each day. I remember the first word, "ti-je-ras" (scissors), suggested as he watched me snipping bandages. He had been in an auto accident, acquiring several injuries, among them a broken arm. He was very courteous and tolerant of discomfort, but having been unconscious when admitted he did not realize that his arm was broken or understand why it was in a rigid cast.

After silently enduring several days in the cast, he summoned me to his bedside. Carefully choosing the somewhat unfamiliar English words, he said, "Doctor, you have been very kind, and I thank you for it. But you've got this arm tied up till I can't use it."

I liked the Mexicans. I found them to be friendly, understanding, appreciative, and very tolerant of my shortcomings. They tended to be of two types: one, the nervous, apprehensive individual showing the impulsive quickness of his spanish ancestry, and the other, more stolid and quiet, showing the unruffled stoicism of Indian ancestry.

I learned that to live in south Texas before air-conditioning I had to be able to tolerate heat. My surgical service started in July. The operating room was like a furnace. Fans were taboo because they stirred up dust. The only respite from the heat was obtained briefly when, after scrubbing hands and forearms, we plunged up to the elbows in vertical tanks of cool, pure alcohol before drying and putting on surgical gloves. After more than fifty years I well remember how wonderful that cool alcohol felt.

For anesthesia we used mostly open-drop ether. The open drop was a joke. In that heat ether evaporated so fast that a drop-by-drop method on the mask would never knock anyone out. We had to pour it on in a small, steady stream.

During ether induction, as the patient begins to lose consciousness, the body may suddenly struggle vigorously against the insult of the ether. Thus before any general anesthesia is contemplated the patient is securely strapped down to prevent his falling off the table or kicking some of the sterile setup. This excitement stage usually lasts only one or two minutes and is not regarded by the anesthetist with any particular apprehension.

But one day when I had pulled anesthesia duty, there was plenty of apprehension. Our man was a muscular giant, a man of obvious great strength, and when he entered the excitement stage things happened. Despite my efforts to restrain him, he sat up. Our sturdy restraining straps went "pop, pop, pop" and he stood up. He seemed to think he was in a fight. Perhaps he was a professional fighter. He took a couple of staggering steps, swinging his fists viciously. Down went the Mayo stand, scattering our sterile instruments. But nothing scattered faster than the surgical crew. All thought of sterile technique vanished as surgeons, nurses, orderlies, everyone fled in panic. That man's fists were big!

I felt that I had to stay. He was my responsibility. I began talking in what I hoped was a soothing voice, calling him by name and reminding him of where he was. Presently he relaxed and obeyed my suggestion that he lie down. He even tolerated the mask when I again explained its function. But this time I grabbed the chloroform bottle. Chloroform acts quickly, and we successfully bypassed the excitement stage as I switched back to ether, the safer anesthetic agent. The crew slunk back in with a fresh setup, and we were in business. Our surgery then proceeded smoothly. Later the patient had no recollection of his exciting behavior.

A nice black man presented with what we felt was a ruptured appendix. He had an obvious surgical belly so was soon shunted to the operating room. The appendix, though badly inflamed, was not ruptured. Then where was all the exudate coming from? Exudate is a murky fluid produced in a contaminated area. Further exploration revealed a perforated ulcer of the duodenum, leakage from which was starting an abscess near the appendix. Here was a dramatic example that multiple pathological conditions may coexist, a good reminder for us young surgeons.

Surgical rounds next evening included, of course, a stop at this patient's bedside. Appreciating that his convalescence was painful, I asked whether he thought he could sleep. "I ain't slepp any yet. It's that fella over in the corner, Doctah. Every time I get 'most asleep he'll fetch a turrible screech and wake me up. But he's been quiet now for a spell, and if I can jes' git a little lead on 'im maybe I'll be all right."

The next day I heard him explaining to relatives the rectal and nasogastric tubes we had inserted to draw off gas. "That Doctah Cook, he got this long skinny little tube and pushed it through my nose and way on down deep in my insides. Then he took a big tube and rammed it up my rear end and tried to meet that little tube."

Had I actually been able to accomplish this feat as he described it, our problems with gas would surely have been solved.

After several days of being fed only by the intravenous route, our man complained cautiously of hunger pains, especially when the food cart passed him by. "Doctah," he pleaded, "I don't see a thing on that li'l wagon that'd hurt me 'ceptin' maybe the china plates. I might get down one too many of them."

Soon thereafter the li'l wagon was permitted to stop regularly at his bedside—and without the loss of any plates.

Stab wounds of the abdomen were our most frequent indication for exploratory surgery. A slender stiletto may make a skin wound less than an inch long and still cause multiple lacerations of the intestines. Or a ridiculously trivial-looking puncture wound made by an ice pick may cause a fatal peritonitis. Bullet wounds, too, we saw almost daily, and they required exploration because they usually punched holes in the intestines. This plethora of accidents afforded us great opportunity to hone our skills in the repair of damaged viscera, training that was for me a great confidence builder and the basis of my later success as a surgeon in private practice.

Nine

One of our fellow interns at the Greene was fortunate enough to have a father who was a doctor and who taught him many things. On one occasion, however, the son felt that the teaching experience was disappointing. John was in medical school at the time, so the old doctor thought it appropriate to give him some firsthand experience in obstetrics. He took him on a home delivery.

Modesty at that time bordered on the ridiculous. On home deliveries, in order that the patient not be embarrassed by exposure, the vulvar area was customarily covered with a sheet. The old doctor accomplished the delivery almost entirely by feel, leaving the sheet in place throughout.

On returning home, the old doctor, proud of his tutelege, asked, "Well, Son, did you learn anything?"

"Yes, Daddy," said John. "I learned you can't see a damn thing through a sheet."

The father, an old country practitioner, was accustomed to rough conditions. He had delivered one of his obstetric patients on a goatskin on the floor, apparently the same goatskin on which the child had been conceived, as no bed was in evidence. He said that being on his knees throughout the delivery was extremely fatiguing.

Another difficult situation developed when he was summoned to attend a woman who was critically ill with pneumonia. As soon as he entered the house, the patient's husband closed and locked the door. "You're not leavin' till morning, Doc," he announced grimly. Then picking up a shotgun, he added, "And if she dies, you do too."

I was surprised at the volatility of tempers in the South. The people were actually not far removed from dueling days when defense of honor was paramount. They were quick to respond aggressively to any potentially hostile situation, and this tendency still permeated John's family. John told me of a few incidents. One concerned a possibly psychotic youth who pursued a girl right into the old doctor's office. She was shrieking for help. "When Daddy saw them," related John, "he grabbed the big shillelagh he keeps behind the door for cases like this, and he knocked the young man down. When I heard all the ruckus I rushed in, and there was Daddy with one foot on the guy's neck, and wavin' the shillelagh. He was gonna brain him. I shouted, 'Don't kill 'im, Daddy!'"

"'He *needs* killin!' Daddy grunted, raising the shillelagh to brain him.

"I stuck out my leg to ward off the blow, and Daddy dang near broke my leg! Then I persuaded him to call the sheriff."

Another incident John related involved a prowler whom John's brothers suddenly discovered on the second floor of the home. As they were dragging the intruder down the stairs, the old doctor began hastily loading cartridges into his revolver. His wife fluttered nervously about, evidently fearing a mess on the carpet. "Now, Smith," she commanded. (She always called him by his last name.) "Now, Smith! Don't kill him in the house. Don't kill him *in the house!*"

Apparently calmer emotions prevailed. Someone called the sheriff, thus sparing both the victim and the carpet.

I was tolerated by John's family and others out of courtesy, but I was openly referred to as the "damn Yankee." Although this was spoken mostly in jest, I could detect some underlying resentment. Only seventy years had elapsed since the Civil War, and considering the agonizing social changes that were forced on the South, it is easy to appreciate why some resentment still lingered. The South was far from being blameless, yet its postwar humiliation was excruciating, and that to an old southerner was almost worse than death.

So I could understand being the "damn Yankee" even though I didn't particularly like it. It emphasized their feeling that I didn't really belong. John and I became close friends, however, and I'm sure he felt little if any resentment toward me.

A deer hunt with John and his friends, however, did little to lessen the friends' resentment when I was the only one to bag a deer. We had left John's house at dawn, carrying sandwiches his mother had provided, bacon between pancakes. I was armed with an old rifle I had rented from a pawnshop the day before. There had been no opportunity to "sight it in," making me wonder whether the sights might be high or low.

Somewhere in the mesquite forest and brush near Uvalde we separated, something I don't like doing with people whose gun-handling habits I do not know. Loving the outdoors as I do, I felt exhilarated, escaping for a time the confining walls of the hospital. I had never before hunted deer with a gun, preferring a camera, or perhaps just stalking to see how close I could get. As a boy I had spent every hour possible in the mountains west of Boulder, Colorado; thus I was thrilled at being again in the woods with all the refreshing early-morning odors. Before long I discovered a game trail, and, selecting a spot of concealment that commanded a view of an open space, I settled down to wait.

In a surprisingly short time along came a deer, head up sniffing the air, ears flicking cautiously, but not detecting the man who was about to murder him. He was in my sights. I hesitated. He was enjoying the beauties of the morning even as I was. I almost hated myself as I pulled the trigger, but alas, the pride and vanity of the hunter overcame compassion.

As it turned out, none of the others got a shot. Thereafter I was not merely the "damn Yankee," I was the "damn Yankee with the rented gun." I have shot only one other deer in my life. That was on a ranch in Wyoming when the roads were blocked with snow, and we needed the meat. I have worked too hard at preserving life to enjoy killing anything. Controlled deer hunting is not a bad thing, however, because overpopulation results in starvation.

Back at the hospital John had an embarrassing experience. It was about a week after he had operated on a woman named Campos for appendicitis. The chief of surgery was making rounds with John, and since it was time for her stitches to come out, the chief expressed a desire to see her incision. John, being justifiably proud of his work, confidently removed the dressing—and disclosed a wound crawling with maggots! That John was in no way to blame for the maggots did little to relieve his shock and embarrassment.

A little pus drainage had encouraged their presence, and there they were, happily crawling about, unconcerned over the revulsion their presence created. Actually their presence may be beneficial. They seldom bother living tissue, feeding instead on dead tissue and pus. Yet their presence is revolting, and the patient feels that he or she is being eaten alive by worms.

Speaking of worms reminds me of the occasional case of hookworm we saw in Texas. Many underprivileged people who were accused of being just plain lazy were actually having their strength sapped by hookworm infestation. It usually occurred in people who went barefoot. The larvae, often found in the mud of swamps and river bottoms, would burrow through the thin skin between the victim's toes, enter the bloodstream, and wind up in the intestine, where they sucked blood. If present in moderate numbers, they caused anemia, fatigue, and lack of ambition.

We advised these poor people to wear shoes so that their feet would be protected. Accordingly, we would sometimes see them going fishing, shoes dutifully slung about their necks—the "charm" that would protect them from hookworm.

One of the busiest doctors in San Antonio was of Mexican descent. Many of the Mexican population naturally preferred him. He was very competent in both medicine and surgery although he was not above catering occasionally to his patients' superstitions.

He was a frugal man in some ways. He encouraged his patients to use empty medicine bottles to bring in their urine specimens so that he could sterilize them and re-use them for dispensing medicine.

One bottle, after sterilization, must have sat on the shelf without a stopper, permitting a large spider to crawl inside, a spider that was not visible through the dark glass when medicine was added.

The man who received this bottle was understandably upset. He had swallowed several doses before the spider appeared. Forgetting his usual awe of the doctor, he rushed back to the office and complained vociferously in front of a reception room crowded with patients.

With complete savoir-faire Dr. U. listened to his tirade, then smilingly punctured his balloon by explaining, "I was afraid that if I told you the spider was in there you might not take the medicine. That's 'Tarantula Tonic,' one of my special formulas. I surely hope you didn't dump it out!"

Even Dr. U. was amazed at the result. People began clamoring for his tarantula tonic. Why fight success? From then on he was buying spiders from all the small boys in the neighborhood.

Ten

He was a quiet man, patient and courteous. After fifty-five years I still remember his name: William B. Rutherford. With one hand wrapped in a bloody towel he was stoically awaiting his turn. There was nothing unusual about that in our emergency room, but when I cautiously unwrapped his hand I was shocked. The function of the hand had been destroyed by the teeth on the revolving cylinder of a cotton gin. Four deep parallel gashes coursed obliquely across the palmar surface of the hand and fingers. Tendons were severed in many places, their torn, ragged ends hanging out, along with damaged nerves, muscles, bones, and blood vessels. It was indeed a gruesome mess.

The man was trying to be philosophical about the expected amputation as he was being readied for the operating room. I was especially thankful that Dr. Pagenstecher, our chief of surgery, agreed to come out. I was relieved that this highly skilled surgeon would be supervising me and, as it turned out, actually doing most of the work.

After hours of tedious repair, including the threading of tendons back through their tunnels, the approximation of the ends of severed nerves, and the realignment of bones, Dr. Pagenstecher finally backed away and threw off his gown.

"Well, Cook," he rumbled, "now it's up to you and God!" This preferential billing made me uncomfortable.

As Dr. Pagenstecher was donning his street clothes, he suddenly stopped with one leg still not in his pants.

"You know, Cook, we are going to try something. It'll be our necks if it doesn't work, because it's experimental, so don't tell anyone. I've got some stuff at the office that I just imported from Germany. It's called Prontosil, and it's supposed to prevent infection. After all our work that poor devil will probably get nothing better than a claw hand because infection will scar all those tendons down like cement. If we can just hold infection down to a minimum, he *could* get a fairly useful hand. I'm going to bring that stuff out. We'll remove the labels so you can just give it a number, and order it on the chart by that number, one ampule every four hours. If the nurses want to know what they're giving, just tell 'em it's a concoction of mine to promote healing."

I was about to become a party to giving some under-the-table medication. I didn't know whether to be excited or worried, so I compromised and was both.

Nor did I have long to wait for the first ill effects of the experimental medicine to appear. A concerned call from the nurse's station informed me that Mr. Rutherford was passing blood in his urine. Oh, boy! The stuff must be highly nephrotoxic! I hastened to the ward. He looked all right, but his specimen was surely red. Was it blood? No, it was red dye from the red prontosil. Mr. Rutherford was apparently not going to die of kidney failure.

A couple of days later I changed the dressings. No pus. Most encouraging. A few days later, still no pus. Dr. Pagenstecher was ecstatic.

"The stuff is working!" he crowed. And it was. In a few weeks Mr. Rutherford was getting pretty good use of his hand, including finger movement except for one finger which was frozen in extension. At his insistence I finally amputated the distal segment of this finger because of its stiffness. He brushed off this minor loss as being inconsequential, as indeed it was in view of the magnitude of his injury. He was so pleased with his restored hand that he asked me to thank our supporting surgical team so they could share in the euphoria of our success. The satisfaction derived from this happy outcome helped to generate in me the stamina required of an intern at the Robert B. Greene. I was glimpsing Father's vision.

Most holidays were obliterated by work. Thanksgiving Day found me pulling day duty in the ER, the busiest place. By four P.M. I was famished, having had only coffee at breakfast. The work was slacking off a bit, encouraging me to anticipate some Mexican food at Chico's across the street. Then came a call from the switchboard. Someone wanted to talk to me. A patient's relatives, no doubt with lengthy questions. I hastened up there, distressed at the idea of having to postpone food even longer.

Imagine my surprise at seeing Mr. Rutherford. And my surprise doubled when he uncovered a large tray revealing a complete Thanksgiving dinner: turkey and dressing, potatoes and gravy all still hot, plus cranberry sauce, salad, milk, and pumpkin pie! Our patients were impoverished. This just did not happen.

Mr. Rutherford spoke: "Four months ago, Doctor, when I was in the hospital I often saw you working right through mealtimes, and I thought that today you might have missed your Thanksgiving dinner." What a delight! The dinner was as delicious as it was welcome. One never knows where gratitude may suddenly appear or what form it may take.

A few weeks after we had labored over Mr. Rutherford's hand, one of our nurses became critically ill with pneumonia. She was young, vivacious, beautiful, good-natured, competent, everything desirable, and she was dying. Everyone loved her, but love, oxygen, and conventional treatment were not doing it. She was comatose, obviously on the verge of death. Doctors and nurses were slipping in frequently to console the unfortunate intern who had drawn women's medical ward duty for the month. It was up to him to sit there and watch her die. Her home must have been far away, as none of her family had appeared. All staff doctors and interns were scouring their brains for an idea that might help.

Suddenly I cursed myself as an idiot. I hurried in and told the attending intern about Dr. Pagenstecher's Prontosil. I noted tears in his eyes as he blurted out, "My God, Cook, we've got nothing to lose! Let's try it." Rushing to a phone, I learned that Dr. Pagenstecher did indeed have some left. He would send it out immediately. And he did. But by the time were able to shoot it into our pitiful patient she had developed a death rattle in her labored breathing. Fever was 106°. Although she was small (perhaps one hundred pounds), we doubled the dose on the first two injections. In her germ-ridden body it was truly kill or cure.

During the next twenty-four hours many of the hospital personnel peeked in, usually with the same question: "You mean she's still alive??" Another two days and the whole place was rejoicing. Amy would live! And live she did, a complete, joyful recovery.

The year was 1936. And what was in that miracle medicine, that Prontosil? What *was* that stuff? We were experiencing our personal introduction to sulphanilamide. It could not have come at a better time!

Eleven

Superstition was ever-present, surfacing colorfully in many areas, especially in obstetrics. The Mexican girls in the last month of pregnancy would tie a string, cord, or belt snugly around the waist above the bulging uterus "to keep the pains from going up." This precaution was considered essential since if the pains should "go up" it was very apt to be fatal both to mother and child. I was spared the need for handling such a disaster because you can be sure I never removed the protective band. Thus I never found out how high the pains might go.

One girl admitted in active labor experienced a cessation of cramps after being comfortably bedded in the hospital. Following several hours of watching this inaction, I was considering sending her home. She might go several days before resuming labor. Her family was disappointed.

To save me the embarrassment of displaying ignorance in front of the family, the grandmother led me to a secluded area. "Doctah, do you know how to start up the pains again?" she queried. Evidently she assumed that my expertise did not extend that far, for without waiting for my reply, she continued quickly, "You jes' go out an' find a old hornet's nes', an' you set fahr to it an' you throw it on the bed, fahr and all. That'll fetch the pains!"

Don't jeer. The stunt would probably work. It would create such panic it might bring all sorts of action, labor pains included.

Another curious superstition that was accepted by many as fact was that the wearing of her husband's hat by a woman in labor would assure a minimum of complications. Hats were therefore often seen in the labor room. One young woman seemed very apprehensive despite having her husband's hat jammed well down over her ears. As her anxiety mounted, she signaled for me to come closer so we could have a moment of confidence. The cause of her anxiety became apparent as she whispered a question in my ear: "Will the hat work just as well if this ain't my husband's child?"

I assured her at once that it would, and she was visibly relieved that the benefits of the hat would not be withheld.

Obstetrics at the Greene was a busy service. Birth control was apparently a "no-no." Rapidity of propagation was exemplified by a statement one of the interns insisted was given him when he asked a woman the ages of her children: "I got a nurser, a lap young'n, one porcher, an' a yard runner."

It was seldom indeed that I opposed the staff doctors at the Greene. They were too knowledgeable to be challenged very often. On one occasion, however, I objected to an order from the acting chief of obstetrics. She insisted that I order a one-gallon enema of hot Epsom salt solution on a woman in eclampsia (toxemia with convulsions). "She has troubles enough without that," I countered.

"They're using it successfully in Ireland," she said loftily.

"I prefer not to blow up the bowel with a gallon of anything," I reasoned. "That's torture." The fact that I had little else to offer in the way of active treatment weakened my position, yet I've always held to the axiom, "If you can't help, at least do no harm."

Happily, with conservative supportive treatment the patient's convulsions ceased, and she had her baby, without regard for what was going on in Ireland.

I recall one most unfortunate incident that occurred when Harry, a fellow intern, was on OB service. I feel that it happened because we were worked to the point of exhaustion. Harry complained of being completely beat so I suggested that we go over to

Chico's and relax a bit. He said, "OK. But I just admitted a girl with a small pelvis. She's eight and half months along and should be induced so her baby won't get too big."

He came back presently from the OB ward, saying, "I left orders to induce labor. I ordered 1 cc of pit, to be increased by 1 cc every twenty minutes till she starts in labor."

"You mean minims of course," I corrected (drops, not cc).

"Yes, minims," he replied. Then horrified, he exclaimed, "My God! You don't suppose I ordered cc, do you?"

Terrified, he rushed back to the ward only to find that he had indeed ordered cc instead of minims (fifteen times his intended dosage), and the nurse had blindly followed his orders without questioning what no doctor in his right mind would have ordered. She had given the first dose, one full cc of pituitrin.

It was certainly working. The patient was having labor contractions that threatened to split the uterus. Before long the cervix had completely dilated, and the baby was jammed tightly into the mother's contracted pelvis.

Harry phoned the chief of the OB service, who dropped everything and came out. They had a difficult struggle, eventually getting a dead baby. Harry's self-recriminations were so severe that I had great difficulty consoling him. There was no real assurance that the baby could have survived the passage through that contracted birth canal anyway. The mother should have had a caesarean section. Yet at that time C-sections often were shunned as indicating ineptitude on the part of the accoucheur. They were accompanied by a higher mortality then than now. In some hospitals, if they had already experienced the estimated "allowable" percentage of caesareans for the year, it was very difficult to crowd in another. It would look bad in their statistics. Happily, that attitude has been discarded. Cases are discussed now by the medical staff and given appropriate individual consideration.

Although the above-described disaster did occur, as it possibly might anywhere, our results were usually very good. Being constantly aware of the high level of responsibility that was thrust upon us, we were conscientious in what we attempted and in our follow-up. It put us on our mettle.

As an example of responsibility I'm thinking of an evening when I was waiting for Dr. Poppen, another intern, to accompany me on a stroll downtown. He was on obstetrics service and was in the delivery room. Apologizing for being delayed, he said, "I'll be a bit longer here than I thought, Cook. I've got an arm down. I'll have to do a podalic version." (This meant reaching up internally and rotating the baby to a foot-first position.)

I couldn't avoid comparing his very casual acceptance of this dangerous complication with how the situation would be handled in the large teaching hospitals. All available interns and residents would probably be called to observe the handling of this major problem. Perhaps even the chief of staff would be summoned for supervision.

An "arm down" meant that the infant's arm was (or soon would be) pushing out as the presenting part. This forces the head to be angled back one way and the body another—an impossible obstacle to delivery. Without appropriate intervention, both mother and baby die. Two options are available, a caesarean or a version.

With no such thing as antibiotics, Dr. Poppen was afraid of infection with a C-section since here it would necessitate dragging a contaminated arm up through an open, vulnerable abdomen. Poppen opted for the version, although there was some danger of infection with that procedure too, but properly accomplished, it was much less shocking to the mother, thus leaving her better able to combat complications.

After waiting for the mother to relax under anesthesia, Dr. Poppen scrubbed the birth canal and the exposed arm with antiseptic, then gently pushed the arm clear back up into the uterus and groped for a foot. Sounds easy. Just grab a foot. But would you believe, it takes discriminating palpation to differentiate toes from fingers in that confusingly cramped space?

Poppen was able to identify a foot and bring it down. A bit later, the other foot, thus proceeding with a normal breech delivery.

Several years before this incident a Dr. Potter, in Buffalo I believe, was performing podalic versions on nearly all of his obstetric cases, after first doing a manual dilatation of the cervix. He wrote a book defending this revolutionary concept, even recommending it. In his skilled hands the maneuver was apparently yielding good results (according to his own reports). None of the recognized authorities agreed with his thinking, however, and his recommendations died with him, to the benefit, I believe, of the childbearing women of the world and their babies.

I recently gave my copy of Potter's book to our son as a historical curiosity.

Twelve

Food at the Greene was nourishing and plentiful, but its palatability, like that of most institutional cuisine, seemed to decline with the passage of time. Each day of the week had its own inflexible menu. Every Tuesday found me struggling valiantly to develop a taste for scrambled brains and eggs. Telling myself that scrambled brains made a delicious meal didn't seem to help. Besides, I hated being so deceitful. So Tuesdays would often find me (and others) at Chico's.

I don't know how I've come this far without greater mention of Chico's place. A letter I wrote home describes it:

As I write I'm seated on Chico's front porch sipping on a straw, with its other end submerged in root beer. Chico and his wife have converted their cottage into an informal Mexican cafe, located directly across the street from the front door of the hospital. There are two tables indoors and two on the porch. Completely unpretentious, like some humble pub, Chico's is an institution. Here is the refuge of the oppressed, the rendezvous of lovers (not guilty yet. Heck!), gossip center extraordinaire and haven of those tired of hospital fare. Here one can obtain a cup of good coffee and a doughnut for five cents— additional sinkers at the rate of one cent each. Dos tacos for cinco centavos; cuatro enchiladas, dix centavos, etc. Also available, such all-time American favorites as ham and eggs.

Chico, himself, is a character. Like a bartender he assumes the role of confidant and philosopher as he listens to our gripes about the hospital. In his white apron and white pill-box cap he almost struts as he serves his tasty specialties. Any comments good or bad about the food Chico accepts as compliments, perhaps giving them a humorous twist such as he did last night when I suggested that he put a bit less pepper in his preparations. With a sly smile he immediately passed me the pepper. "You say you wanta more pepper?"

Since the hospital call bells can be heard from across the street, being on call does not deprive us of the occasional interlude at Chico's, so here I am relaxing and too tired to pay much attention to the assaults of all the things that creep, crawl, and fly around me. They're mostly moths, yet I shouldn't fail to mention a nondescript kitten that persists in scaling my pants leg. Being an old climber myself, I can scarcely find heart to discourage him. Dr. Speer, a fellow intern, is with me. He has been commenting on his difficulty in understanding Spanish, a real handicap at the Greene. When Chico appeared with coffee, he noticed his dog lying by one of the tables, and he gave a command to the animal in Spanish. The dog obediently arose and walked out. "There!" Speer exclaimed. "Doesn't that make you feel stupid? Even the dogs understand it."

Speer's sense of humor prompted him to relate part of a conversation he claimed to have had with a very elderly patient. In recording her history he was trying to uncover any past illnesses of consequence. Her memory was sluggish until he asked, "Have you ever been bedridden?"

"Oh, lots of times, Sonny," she replied, suddenly coming to life. "And twice in a buggy!"

A week or two in the venereal disease clinic came close to frightening me into celibacy. In addition to syphilis and gonorrhea, we saw granuloma inguinale, lymphogranulo venereum, and soft chancre. This last one is often confused with syphilis, although the treatment is quite different. Gonorrhea was the leader in frequency, and at that time we could never be sure of a cure. Those other bad actors with the big names we saw less often.

One young man entering the general clinic gave his self-diagnosis as "woman trouble." The alert and experienced receptionist correctly referred him to the venereal disease clinic.

A girl of fifteen, another gonorrhea victim, made the following statement: "My sister said to me, 'You're fifteen now. It's time to get your ass out there on the front step and bring in some money.'"

We were constantly swept from the trivial to the tragic. A woman explained that she had very conscientiously been rubbing some kind of "ornament" on the "garter" on her neck, but she finally concluded that she must be using the wrong kind of "ornament" because the goiter was not regressing.

A mother brought in a four-year-old daughter whose behavior seemed strange. She wore a vacant, almost unseeing stare as she fingered the furniture and crawled under the chairs. "Jes' look at that child," the mother commented. "She's got some kind of miraculous misery." Her "misery" turned out to be more syphilitic than miraculous. It was congenital syphilis of the central nervous system, at that time a fatal condition.

An eighteen-month-old infant was brought in with high fever. How high? Just over 110. It was perhaps just as well that the child did not survive, as fever of that magnitude is expected to cause brain damage. The mother, while shopping, had left the baby in the car with windows rolled up on a hot Texas day, not realizing that the temperature in the car would probably reach 160 degrees.

As previously mentioned, we encountered superstition almost daily, some harmful, some amusing, some possibly helpful, and some very pitiful like that displayed by a poor, uneducated young mother who sought help for her six-week-old baby. The child was thin, dehydrated, and the color of raw pie dough. The mother finally realized that things were going badly even though she was following diligently the instructions she received from her mother, the child's grandmother. "Is the baby breast-fed?" I asked.

"No, I kinda dried up. Since she's been sick I've been careful to do exactly what Momma told me to do. I've been givin' her nothin' but chicken-manure tea, from only the white part of the chicken manure. That's what you make the tea with, just the white part."

"She'll need more than that now," I said gently, as I made arrangements for a hasty admission. One more day and the infant would have been dead. In the hospital we had nutrients available that were definitely superior to chicken manure, even the white part. The baby slowly recovered but was not dismissed until the young mother was instructed in infant feeding.

Infant feeding reminds me of an incident (possibly fictitious) that was told on one of the interns in the pediatric clinic. A young woman presented a baby which she felt was not getting enough to eat. The intern asked whether the infant was breastfed. The answer was "Yes."

"Let me see your breasts, please," he asked, whereupon the young woman exposed her breasts for his inspection. After careful palpation of the breasts, first one, then the other, he announced, "It's no wonder the baby is hungry. You seem to have no milk."

"It's my sister's baby," she explained. Then looking with increasing interest at the handsome young doctor, she added mischievously, "But I'm glad I came."

We are inclined to think of mammograms as something relatively new, and indeed there have been improvements in techniques, but we were doing mammograms at the Greene over fifty years ago. We used air contrast in some, too, injecting air into the breast to make use of the fact that a nodule, being denser than air, would cast a shadow.

Young women especially seemed delighted with the resulting full contour when the breasts were full of air. On noting the saucy upward tilt achieved by the air, they often would ask hopefully, "Will they stay like this?" We felt mean to disappoint them, but the provocative new contour was, of course, temporary.

Thirteen

One of our hospital patients made his living by selling live rattlesnakes to zoos and to special laboratories that used the venom. On the day of his admission he had been less lucky than usual. He had been bitten, not by the snake he was catching with his loop but by another which he had not seen as it lay hidden under a ledge of rock.

He said, "I went ahead and caught the snake I was after. Then I caught the one that bit me. And on the way to the pickup I caught another one. When I got back to the house, I dropped the gunny sack full of snakes by the snake house and headed for town. Then I realized that those snakes in the sack would die in the hot sun, so I turned around and went back to put 'em in the snake house. It has a shade roof over it like a tent fly. Then I came on in."

His bite was just above the knee, and by the time he reached the hospital his leg was twice normal size. His pulse was racing, and he was becoming short of breath. But he was tough and recovered quickly enough to be dismissed in a few days.

Before his departure, he invited me out to see his snakes. "I'll show you snakes that are as big around as your leg above the knee." This statement I discounted as gross exaggeration until I visited his snake house. He had 'em!

The snake house was a shed about ten by twelve feet. There was a center aisle about three feet wide with cages of heavy mesh screen stacked three deep on either side, and most of these cages contained snakes. When we stepped on the front porch, a great buzzing roar started up inside. Walking down the narrow aisle was a bit unnerving. There was a recurrent bumping sound on either side as the big snakes struck their heads against the screen in an attempt to bite.

I squatted down near floor level to stare at one big fellow who seemed to be glaring quietly at me. I moved my hand close to the cage to see whether I was quick enough to jerk away before his head hit the wire mesh. I couldn't get him to strike at my hand. He seemed indifferent to my challenge as we tried to stare each other down. Finally deciding that he was not going to move, I glanced away and withdrew my hand. Bam! His head hit the screen. He knew the moment I relaxed my guard, and he waited for that moment to strike. I would have been nailed.

I turned to see that the snake hunter had removed a big snake from a cage and was holding it by the neck, evidently for my edification. "Show the nice man your fangs, Bertha," he said as he pried her mouth open. I could see drops of venom dripping from the tips of her fangs, vicious hypodermic needles. The snake hunter, a very muscular man, had all he could handle in controlling Bertha's powerful coils. She was indeed as big as my leg above the knee. He soon flipped her back into the cage and slammed the door.

Of the snakebite victims who reached the hospital alive during the time when I was at the Greene, we lost only one, a five-year-old girl who had the misfortune to be one hundred miles from the hospital when bitten. She was in extremis on arrival and died soon after.

Another victim was dead on arrival. He had picked up a stick and struck at a huge snake in a grape vineyard, an assault the snake evidently felt was unsportsmanlike. Instead of trying to escape, as a snake ordinarily would, this one was so fighting mad that it rushed the man and bit him. Now it was the man's turn to attempt escape, but when he turned to flee, his feet became entangled in downed grapevines, causing him to fall almost at once. On came the snake, not wishing to lose this advantage, and as the man jumped up to run, the snake bit him twice more.

This was the story we obtained from the victim's friends who brought him in. He had walked a mile for help but died before reaching the hospital.

During my subsequent practice in Nebraska, I found the Great Plains rattlers to be much smaller and their bite rarely fatal. And after training at the Greene I felt little anxiety in handling snakebite. The Greene was reputed to treat more rattlesnake bites than any other facility in the world.

I haven't mentioned insect bites and stings or spider bites, some of which can be significant, especially where allergy is involved. Most of the bites that came to our attention were black widow and brown recluse spiders. Tarantula bites were extremely rare and not as dangerous as commonly supposed. The brown recluse is worse. Its bite usually produces a festering sore that is slow to heal.

One day as I was reflecting on spider bites, a young black woman caught my attention. "Doctah, I got bit."

Immediately a black widow came to mind—the most frequent. "What bit you?" I asked.

She extended a swollen arm. "I got bit by a woman!" a more dangerous event because of probable infection.

Another bite I was called on to treat proved to be a once-in-a-lifetime experience. Picnic festivities at Brackenridge Park were interrupted one evening when one of the revelers suffered a rare and original accident and was brought in almost sober, with blood all down the front of his pants. One of his supporters explained the accident: "He got this wild idea, and stuck his penis through the bars of the hyenas' cage!"

I was distressed to discover that the entire head of the penis was gone, the stump still bleeding freely. Were this chap in the army, he would now be uniquely eligible for "short arm inspection." He must not have realized that a hyena's jaws can crack the leg bone of a buffalo. Some things are harder than others, male ego notwithstanding. Plastic repair was difficult and not entirely satisfactory, what with the hyena both unwilling and unable to relinquish the missing part.

A few weeks later I visited Brackenridge Park myself. Some curious subconscious association attracted me to the hyenas' cage, but you can be sure I was careful not to poke a finger, or anything, through the bars.

Fourteen

It is difficult to convey to an outsider the frantic activity of the emergency room at the Greene on Saturday nights. It was indeed bedlam. The cases showed incredible variety, but our stock in trade was knife wounds: cuts and stabbings, usually by the Mexicans, and social razor slashings as perfected by the blacks. One of the black boys showed me how to hold the razor—"If you don't want to kill 'im, just mark 'im up real good."

There were beatings and bitings, fistfights and shootings, and withal a scattering of people who were just plain sick. The antithesis of this pandemonium was exemplified one night by a quiet little man who "just stopped in to rest a while." Strange place to try to rest! All benches were occupied by the injured so with a confused sigh he departed. There had to be more restful places.

At almost anytime on a Saturday night you could hear ambulance sirens emanating from different directions. The ambulances were owned and operated by the various funeral parlors in town since accident victims were always possible customers. Competition for bodies was keen.

Formerly, when an emergency call came into police headquarters, it was relayed to all ambulance companies (mortuaries). This created a pell-mell rush to the scene that all too often resulted in a collision of two ambulances at a corner near the accident site. Such collisions became so prevalent that the city fathers divided the city into zones, giving each company responsibility for calls in its assigned zone only. Since some zones were more productive than others, they were rotated so that coverage would be fairly distributed.

The drivers were mostly young Mexicans with more skill than judgment. I rode with one once on a child drowning case. The driver was from Morales mortuary, and he was both fearless and skillful. Of course, over fifty years ago there was far less traffic, but even so as we raced along Alamo Plaza, right downtown, at seventy miles an hour with siren screaming, I was extremely apprehensive.

"Do we have to go this fast, Pepe?" I yelled.

"It don't matter," he shouted back. "I've got TB, and the doctor says I don't have long to live anyway."

If this answer was supposed to reassure me, it didn't. I was visualizing the gory injuries we saw almost daily from shattered windshields. The inventor of shatterproof glass has spared thousands of people severely disfigured faces. Formerly, in any frontal impact, the passenger often went through the windshield, an experience comparable to running the gauntlet past razor-wielding savages.

As it turned out, we were not in time to save the drowned boy, and to this day mention of the Alamo recalls that hell-for-leather ride with the tuberculous Jehu who shattered my equanimity.

It was on Saturday nights in the emergency room that I learned to sew with alacrity and moderate dexterity. Those were the times when the place lived up to its nickname, the "Bucket of Blood." One orderly was kept busy all night just mopping blood off the floor.

The intern on duty would be frantically repairing wounds, trying desperately to keep up with the more serious injuries. But he would be interrupted by the approach of another ambulance. "Time for two or three more stitches before they hit the ramp." Then, as the sound of the wailing siren slid downhill on its final moan, the doctor would interrupt his sewing long enough to run to the door, sterile towel in hand to jam into the site of severest hemorrhage. A quick evaluation would determine the urgency of the situation.

If the newcomer was able to sit up, he would join the group of waiting wounded who were filling up the benches, and perhaps spilling off onto the floor, all holding bloody towels over their wounds.

Tired police officers would be trying to obtain enough information for their reports. A typical situation would go something like this:

Cop, approaching patient on the operating table: "What's your name?" (Silence.) "I said, 'What's your name?' ¿Cómo se llama?"

Patient (after additional interval of aggravating reflection): "José Mendoza."

Cop: "Who cut you?"

Patient: "A friend."

Cop: "What's his name?"

Patient: "I don't know. He's just a friend."

Cop: "If he's a friend, you know his name."

Patient: "No. He's just a friend."

The patient's refusal to identify his assailant was explained to me after the policeman had moved on. "If I tell his name, then they'll put him in jail where I can't get to him. This way you'll see him in here next week."

I recall one very pale and apprehensive man who was holding firm pressure over his two severed external jugular veins with a tightly rolled towel that had been applied by his experienced ambulance driver. After I had ligated the cut veins (others would assume their function), the patient relaxed somewhat. My local anesthesia was minimizing his discomfort.

"Doctor." He spoke up timidly, putting the emphasis on the last syllable. "Doctor, I not die?"

"No, you won't die," I assured him. Then, soon after my reassurance, he became talkative. "Do you know who do this to me?"

I confessed my ignorance.

"My wife, *he* do this to me. Yes, my wife, he do this to me. Every day my wife ask me for a leetle money. He save the money and buy a beeg knife. And when I come home today my wife, he say, 'You look tired. Better you take a nap now.' Then when I go to sleep my wife he sneak in with his new beeg knife and cut my throat Ar-r-rgh! Now, Doctor, what would you do weeth a woman like that?"

"I'm not sure," I replied truthfully. "Where is she now?"

"Oh, he's in jail. Yes," he spoke with apparent satisfaction. "He's in jail."

One unfortunate knife-wound victim suffered an oblique slash through the larynx, exposing and separating the vocal cords. The patient's father was pressing the youth for information, but with the larynx hanging open, speech is impossible.

Without much confidence in the maneuver, I squeezed the larynx together, and surprisingly, while I held the voice box in place, he could talk. A relatively simple repair restored both neck and voice.

I was surprised to find that one of the most frequent accidents to plague women is the breaking off of a sewing machine needle in a finger. Yet it is easy to visualize how it happens. If a finger is under the descending needle, it will be punctured deeply. Instinctive reaction causes the woman to jerk her hand away, thus snapping off the needle in her finger. Removing such fragments under the fluoroscope was one of the procedures that produced latent x-ray burns on my hands, burns that were not detectable until much later, when a skin rash appeared.

Late one night a beautiful young woman of twenty-five was brought to Emergency near death from a self-inflicted bullet wound of the chest. I was silently bemoaning our limited open-chest capabilities when she whispered, "Please, don't try to save me. I have terminal TB. This way is quicker and easier."

She clasped my hand, gave me a sweet smile, and died. Later that night, while I was still endeavoring to accept her death, a gunshot victim came in who cheered me up considerably because the bullet was lodged in the sternum, easily accessible under local anesthesia. I assured the man that he would be fine—that he wouldn't even have to be hospitalized, and as I prattled on euphorically, I wondered why my comments were being received with sullen stoicism. Then a policeman enlightened me. The bullet I was removing had first passed through the patient's son, killing him. I offered sympathy, of course, but the man never uttered word one.

Again I felt depressed. It was not a happy night. I wished I were in the lobby of the old Menger Hotel watching the alligators and trying somehow to share their lethargic tranquillity, their freedom from care. They were in a pit with water, something of a tourist attraction. Their inactivity had a hypnotic influence that favored relaxation.

Not far from the Menger is the famed Alamo, with its small park, where I was occasionally privileged to walk or sit in the moonlight with a nurse who didn't mind walking the mile from the hospital. On ten dollars a month you don't drive a car or even go to a movie very often.

Sometimes at the hospital we would climb a steel ladder inside the top of the elevator shaft to get on the roof, where there was privacy and perhaps moonlight. Or a walk along the San Antonio River could be interesting, although the river walk was not developed as it is today. Yet there were a few short stretches where one (or two) could walk.

Fifteen

If we expected the unusual at the Greene, we were seldom disappointed, and unfortunately some of these surprises were tragic. There was the young man who must have had a pretty serious altercation with his wife. He decided to drop in on her unexpectedly. He hired an airplane pilot to fly him over their house, with the expectation of giving his wife a nasty surprise. Without having the advantage of a Norton bombsight, he did rather well, missing the mark by only two houses. He was out of the plane before the astonished pilot could restrain him.

In a house two doors from his home, preparations for supper were just being completed when a sudden splintering crash disrupted everything. The supper table disappeared, dishes and all, as the dejected neighbor completed his descent in their midst.

Much of his clothing was ripped off as he passed through the roof and ceiling, but the shreds that were left contained an unimaginable number of wood splinters. The same was true of the skin. He looked like a porcupine, except for his face, which miraculously had not a scratch.

Through this sky-diving act, our man no doubt hoped that his wife would be struck by the power of his emotions. It would be a lesson to her. It evidently was a lesson to him, too, since I'm sure he never attempted it again.

As he was being transferred to the mortuary, a helpful neighbor rushed in with a shoe that had been lost in the fall. It was surprisingly heavy. There was a foot in it.

Some emergencies were medical in nature. I recall checking a woman with a severe breathing problem. One look at her throat suggested membranous tonsillitis, or perhaps that now rare disease, diphtheria. Since she was experiencing partial laryngeal obstruction, I opted for diphtheria. Then I noticed some skin lesions and beginning nasal deformity suggestive of leprosy, so I listed both conditions on her admission slip and sent her to isolation. Since the combination of these two diseases is extremely rare, I was really sticking my neck out. Diphtheria alone was becoming infrequent and leprosy in San Antonio? Don't be ridiculous. The case created quite a flap and made me the butt of much good-natured razzing.

Throat cultures, however, confirmed diphtheria, and with heavy doses of antitoxin she was able to squeak by without a tracheostomy. Then when the lab reported the nasal scrapings positive for leprosy, and she was sent elsewhere for treatment, my fellow interns ceased ribbing me about Cook's new leper colony.

Ignorance or carelessness claimed the life of a house mover. Not being on ER duty, I paid little attention to the approach of another ambulance. Then suddenly I experienced gut-wrenching shudders as a man's screams overrode the moan of the siren—screams interspersed with the most pathetic pleas, "For God's sake, fellas, get me off these wires!"

In a moment of cowardly withdrawal, I felt glad that I was not on emergency room service. Then my call bell rang. The victim was being shunted immediately to surgical service—me!

I rushed to the OR, praying that he would not be as bad off as he sounded. He was worse.

He was a house mover, and he had climbed atop a house to raise a power line so the house could pass under it. Perhaps he had grabbed two wires. At any rate, a powerful current had surged through his arms, probably in one side and out the other, and he could not let go. Lord alone knows how long it took to rescue him, but it was too long. He was cooked—hands and arms turned mostly to charcoal. Fortunately, the poor fellow died that night. We could relieve his pain, nothing more. He must have had the heart of a mule to resist fibrillation in the presence of so much current.

In thinking of something less tragic, I recall a patient on one of the medical wards who could shake things up a bit. His name was Lovie, not Louie, but Lovie, and it seemed appropriate. He insisted on donning his hospital gown backward, and to the nurses' dismay, he refused to tie the strings. The reason for their dismay soon became evident.

Toilet facilities in all early hospitals were grossly inadequate. The buildings must have been designed by architects who, having grown up in the era of outdoor privies, felt that the luxury of one indoor flush toilet per floor was adequate. At the Green we did better. We had one toilet per ward, still not enough.

One ward was constructed like a long, wide hallway with a windowed porch at the far end. A row of eight beds lined each side of the hallway, and there were four beds on the porch. As there were always more women on this ward, they occupied the main room or hallway, while the men were bedded on the porch.

When the male patients became ambulatory, they were expected to walk to the toilet, but to reach it they had to traverse the long hallway between the women's beds. Lovie made this trip a production.

He would stride flamboyantly down the passageway, his gown, unencumbered by any ties, flowing out behind, exposing his generously endowed manhood for all to see and admire, a proud staff or swinging pendulum, depending on his mood.

The women would shriek with dismay (or delight) and cover their heads, usually after he had strutted past. The thing that puzzled me was Lovie's lack of embarrassment over the appearance of his virile but badly battered shaft. It had obviously explored at least one contaminated passage because it exhibited the worst soft chancre deformities I had ever seen. Deep, healed ulcerations had left him terribly scarred, dramatically marred by many gouged-out craters such as might be made with a small ice cream scoop. But Lovie was unabashed. He was proud to display what looked like a kinky piece of driftwood. So every few hours it was "showtime."

We had another exhibitionist who was admitted occasionally to the medical ward. He had the worst case of psoriasis I have ever seen, but he was sufficiently resourceful to have devised a method of using the gruesome condition for entertainment. Visiting hours at the Greene, except for critical cases, were limited to two days a week; hence on these days the rooms and halls were packed with relatives, friends, and curiosity seekers in a milling chaos sufficient to give a fire marshal a nervous breakdown.

Our psoriasis patient could empty those halls and occasionally did so in such a spectacular manner that we were loath to restrain him. Wild-eyed, shrieking and yelling like a banshee, he would explode from his room stark naked, with all of his disfiguring lesions flaunted in plain sight, and he would race among the terrified onlookers, who melted before him like hot butter. They assumed from his awful skin that he must be horribly contagious, and they fled in panic. Once he had dispersed the crowd, he would return quietly to his room to reflect mischievously on the effect of his actions. The caper was one of his few pleasures in life.

On the pediatric ward a surprising number of young children were there because of pneumonia from kerosene poisoning. There's no use asking a kid why on earth he drank the nasty stuff. He doesn't know.

We got so we could diagnose the condition as the child was being carried down the hall because of the strangely characteristic cough that develops, and of course the reek of kerosene would remove all doubt. I never understood how enough of the kerosene got into the lungs to produce the pneumonia, but it obviously did. Thank goodness, with the disappearance of coal-oil lamps, such poisonings are now infrequent, but in those days we saw at least two a week.

We had a little boy on the pediatric ward with coeliac disease. He had been in the hospital for several weeks while we experimented with his diet, so all the nurses and doctors knew him. He was five years old on a three-year-old frame, stunted because of his disease. Everyone liked him and spoiled him because of his cute personality. Somebody on the staff launched him on a career of vagrancy by teaching him to beg for pennies.

One day as Dr. Randall was making rounds, little Jimmy stuck out his hand, demanding a penny. Dr. Randall was not what you might visualize as the typical pediatrician. He was a huge man, standing six feet, four inches tall, with the frame of a fullback. Jimmy was well acquainted with him, and the little guy was not at all frightened when Dr. Randall roared down at him, "My Lord, boy! I gave you a penny just last week. What are you doing with all that money? You must be keeping a woman!"

I hope the following story that was going the rounds on the pediatric ward cannot be authenticated. A doctor who had been spending a good deal of time following the stock market received a call from a distraught mother. "I'm terribly worried about my baby," she said. "His temperature keeps going up. It's up to 104 now."

"If it hits 105," replied the doctor cryptically, "sell."

About one-third of the patients on the pediatric ward looked like little Arabs because of all the gauze wrapped around their heads. They were convalescing from mastoid operations, a procedure that is a rarity now, thanks to antibiotics. But at that time tonsillitis and adenoiditis frequently progressed to ear infection and abscess, which in turn tended to extend into the mastoid sinus behind the ear. If the abscessed sinuses were not opened and cleaned out, the resulting internal pressure and infection might invade the brain.

Now, with antibiotics, tonsillectomy is indicated less frequently, although there are still children who benefit from it. Unfortunately, some well-meaning internists have sought to save the child from the surgeon by condemning tonsillectomy and adenoidectomy as undesirable operations now that we have antibiotics, and at the other extreme, I'll concede the existence of a few surgeons who have operated with minimal indications. But, antibiotics cannot do everything, and some people need tonsils and adenoids removed.

In private practice, the youngest patient on whom we did an adenoidectomy was nine months old. He had never been well, had chronic ear infection, and could not gain weight. He was anemic and very listless. After surgery his ears cleared up. He sprouted like a weed and quickly achieved good health. Except for the very young age, his was not an unusual case. As with most surgery, benefit can be expected to be commensurate with the indication.

Tonsillectomy is classified as minor surgery. Therefore, many people tend to regard it as not very serious, and if all goes well, perhaps it isn't. It also can be scary as hell. Hemorrhage can certainly occur, and the specter of cardiac arrest is ever-present. In fifty years of doing tonsils, I have had cardiac arrest occur twice. Both times the heart was restarted by a sharp blow to the chest and a generous mixture of prayer and good luck. It has been my good fortune never to have had a fatality associated with tonsillectomy.

Hemorrhage as a complication occurs more frequently than we would like, and some degree of expertise may be required to control it. There is an old adage concerning hemorrhage which, although quite true, is not entirely reassuring. It states, "All bleeding eventually stops." That's about as cheering as saying that death is nature's way of suggesting that you slow down (nor original with me).

Of course, we couldn't slow down at the Greene. There was too much work to permit much relaxation. But there was one staff doctor who worked so slowly that I could rest while assisting him in surgery. He thought that no one else could operate as skillfully as he. His paranoid personality should have alerted me that he might be a bit dangerous, but I never would have believed how dangerous. I was working with a mass murderer.

I can mention his name, Dr. Ross, since he was written up in the newspapers of that day and in *Time* magazine. My suspicion that he was a bit paranoid was born out by a subsequent tragedy. He had entrusted all his savings to a friend for investment. Through fraud or mismanagement, the savings disappeared.

Dr. Ross sought revenge in a decisive manner. Knowing when the friend was planning to visit his cabin in the woods, he concealed himself nearby armed with a deer rifle. The fact that the "friend" was accompanied by his wife and three children did not deter Dr. Ross. He opened fire, intending to kill all five. Four died on the spot, but one girl escaped through the woods with Dr. Ross in hot pursuit. It was imperative that he kill her too because she had seen him and knew him from previous contacts. Possibly the doctor lost time in reloading. At any rate, she eluded him, although wounded, and her subsequent testimony put him behind bars.

Sixteen

In any recollections of the Robert B. Greene Hospital I am always drawn to the emergency room because that is the area that seemed consistently colorful.

One Sunday morning, after a typical Saturday night in the ER, I attempted to jot down a listing of the night's activities, thinking such a résumé might be of nostalgic interest at some later date when recalling events at the old hospital. From the stack of patient record cards I came up with the following outline:

Saturday Night, April 17, 1937

Woman in car wreck. Pain in sacral area. To x-ray.

Man stabbed in left forearm and sliced under left nipple.

Man in fight. Two-inch laceration scalp.

While suturing this wound, I hear siren, heralding approach of another ambulance, which unloads three men. Hasty check of these new arrivals shows one with fractured skull. "Miss Renteria, admit this one to Men's Surgical. Tell 'em to be ready with some 50 percent IV glucose and some IM mag sulfate to combat cerebral edema. Other two can wait."

Back to scalp suturing.

An asthmatic staggers in, about to collapse. "Nurse, give that woman ten minims of adrenalin." Another siren is audible, not yet close.

"Doctor, my wife, he is very sick. Will you please help him?"

"As soon as I can, Señor; the ambulance is coming in."

Time for two more stitches before its arrival. The siren is now down to a low, throaty whirr as the ambulance hits the ramp. In rolls a stretcher with a frighteningly bloody figure leaving a trail of red. I jerk the covering towel from his neck and grasp a spurting vessel with an artery clamp. (He'll have to wait a bit.)

Back to stitching the man's head. Three more sutures. "Come to the clinic Friday to get those stitches out. Where's that man's sick wife? I'll see those other two guys in a moment."

"Doctor, look at my arm. I got bit yesterday." I turn and see an area of alarming inflammation around deep imprints of human teeth. "Show this woman the use of hot compresses."

"Doctor, the man in the far bed in the observation room is having a convulsion."

"Fix an ampul of IV sodium amytal."

"My brother was hit on top of the head with a gun barrel."

"Sit down, please, till I finish here."

"Doctor, can the man with the three bullet wounds go home?"

"Was that blood count ordered on Martinez?"

"Doctor, the woman in bed one is having a fainting spell."

"Miss Renteria, please admit this girl. She's in labor. And get someone to give that Rodriguez baby an enema."

"Doctor, here's a patient with a note from Dr. Graves. Can we admit her? There's no diagnosis on the slip."

"Miss R., let's have that fellow in the corner on the table next— the one with the cut neck. He's been waiting a long time."

"Here is my little boy. A dog bit him."

"Some tetanus antitoxin, Miss. R."

Another ambulance, another car wreck. "Doctor, these people will require suturing, but they don't seem badly hurt. I'll have to leave them in the hall for now."

The siren is moaning again. This time it's a toddler who ran in front of a car, plus the man who jumped into the street to save it. Both have only scratches and bruises.

"Doctor, I have two sick men out here." I look up to see a frightened young Mexican in the doorway.

"What happened to them?"

"Their car turn over and they fall out. I think one is dead."

"Clear the table, Miss R., so I can examine this man. His face is a mess. The other one's dead all right. And we'd better take the man with the clamp in his neck next. Admit that child with the burns. We can't handle him here."

Another ambulance. "Put this guy in observation. We'll sew him up when we can get to him. He says the wreck hasn't been reported. Call the police. No, call the sheriff; it happened out of town."

"A woman has fainted out here, and her baby is sick!"

"Check the mother. Bring 'em in if you can, and take the baby's clothes off. I've got a few more stitches here."

An irate wife arrived with a drunk husband. We're pretty busy to nurse drunks. "Walk him around a few blocks."

In come the police. "Doc, we've got a fellow here says he can't get his breath. Where do you want him?"

"We've got 'em on stretchers, benches, and in corners," I replied. "Miss R., move somebody. He'll need to sit. Give him adrenalin. He's having a bad asthmatic attack."

Another ambulance. "We picked this guy up off the street unconscious. He may have been hit by a car."

"Miss R., are you getting cards on all these people?"

Man brought in by girlfriend who became alarmed at the amount of blood that gushed forth after she had stabbed him.

Another ambulance. Victim's car hit by a train. Patient will live. Car perished.

Girl with severe pleurisy pain in car wreck while en route to hospital.

Gunshot wound of patella.

Car wreck. Severe lacerations of face.

Eight months pregnant. Vomiting and cramps.

Car wreck, man has broken ribs.

Man, knife wounds of chest: two ten-inch intersecting slashes.

Splinter of glass deep in thigh. Excised under local.

Knife cuts of face. Twelve sutures.

Beaten up. Balloonlike swelling of face. Cuts, bruises, drunk.

Car wreck. Multiple lacerations of face and neck.

Razor cuts, shoulders and chest.

It must be 7 A.M. I see Jim, my relief man, coming on duty. Jim is an absolutely unshakable little tough guy. He is right in his element wading around in blood in the emergency room, and he's a swell fellow to work with. "Catch that ambulance load coming up the ramp, Jim. I'm pretty busy here. Then I can report on what's in the observation room."

Then, after an hour and a half of catching up, I was suddenly off duty. The above-listed assortment of injuries is not complete, but it gives some idea of the challenge facing the intern on ER duty. He was expected to handle that sort of night with the help of one nurse and an orderly. If the nurse happened to be Miss Renteria, he was lucky.

Having to be penurious myself, I was somewhat jealous of Jim's life-style. He was always in high spirits, living a fuller, more stimulating life, smelling all the flowers, picking life's fruits, loving all the girls—and, damn it—through it all, he managed to be an excellent doctor. One morning about three o'clock, however, he came dragging in, having been to the horse races, followed by other excitement, and for once he looked almost dejected.

"Cook," he said, removing his shoes. "You're looking at a victim of slow horses and fast women." And with that he flopped on the bed.

The urology clinic was messy. I was about to say it was mostly "old men" till I realized that many were younger than my present age. But I'll have to admit to being an old man, having been born in 1911.

Anyway, it was messy. The ward was full of old men, each with a retention catheter. Most were there for prostate surgery. We were working before the invention of the Foley catheter that has an inflatable bulb to hold it in place in the bladder; hence we had to depend on ingenuity and the use of tape strips to secure the catheters in place. Leakage was frequent and irritating.

I'm reminded of my father's comment after his prostate surgery. He had the misfortune to bleed excessively, leaving him weak but still with his sense of humor. He said, "I used to think that people who put that extra 'R' in 'prostate' were making a mistake, but they're not!"

I recall one patient who had been seen in the clinic several times for an intractable cystitis, a somewhat unusual condition for a man in his thirties. He was referred in for cystoscopy when I happened to be handling that service, and I was glad to see a younger patient for a change.

As I was gazing into his bladder with the cystoscope, through the swirling irrigation water, I noted several irritated, slightly hemorrhagic spots on the bladder wall. Suddenly, "What's was that?" A "fence post" had just floated past the end of the scope. I kept searching until I found it again and was able to identify it as a wooden match, greatly magnified. Removing it posed a problem because in order to draw it out through the slender scope, I would have to grasp it by the very tip. Otherwise it would hang up in a crosswise position.

With the appropriate slender alligator forceps I chased the match all around the bladder, finally succeeding in obtaining the necessary angle, and triumphantly extracting my "fence post" through the scope.

On being shown the offending foreign body, the patient felt obligated to explain its presence. He volunteered two possible explanations: (1) "It must have flipped in there when I was splitting wood with an ax"; or (2) "It may have been pushed in there when I saw down hard on a load of kindling."

I accepted these fantastic theories without argument. Little would have been gained by embarrassing the patient further. I suspect that he was experimenting with sensation, since a young man is rarely in need of a wampus (artificial penile splint).

Before leaving the urology clinic I should like to describe that ingenious (and quite imaginary) instrument, the gonophone, used in diagnosing gonorrhea (the clap), that miserable affliction that is caused when the gonococcus germ invades the urethra. The gonophone is a combination stethoscope and cystoscope. After inserting the cystoscope end into the patient's urethra, the examiner plugs the ear pieces into his ears to see if he can hear the gonococci "clapping."

The boys in the Ear, Nose, and Throat Clinic were puzzled by a man who complained of pain in his maxillary sinus area following a bad cold. There seemed nothing unusual about that except that he insisted he was experiencing noise and movement in one side of his face—in his cheek. He was so insistent that something be done that one of the boys cut an opening into the maxillary sinus to drain and irrigate it.

Surprise! He flushed out a batch of maggots. The man was a sheepherder, and he admitted to have gotten drunk and fallen asleep on a hillside above the sheep. Evidently a blowfly selected his snotty nose as an appropriate place to lay eggs. Nosy critter.

Seventeen

My love life in the highly romantic city of San Antonio was restricted by poverty and an excessive workload. Paucity of dating opportunities, however, did not prevent my becoming very fond of Ana. She was a beautiful Aztec nurse with copper-colored skin, expressive dark eyes, and a beautiful personality to match. I was first attracted to her because in the hospital environment of heat, humidity, and sweat she was always sparklingly clean, immaculately starched and fresh, unaffected by her sordid surroundings. She was also intelligent and fun to be with.

She was my companion at the only dance I attended in San Antonio. It was a Mexican dance, in one of the areas from which we drew many of our stabbings. I loved the music, but I didn't conform to the crowd. At six feet I seemed to be the tallest one in the hall, and with blond hair I felt as conspicuous as a burning gas well at midnight. Furthermore, I was squiring one of "their" women, and this aroused hostility.

In the clinic and hospital I got along with Mexicans like old friends, but this was a different arena. And although I was in great shape physically and unaccustomed to running away from confrontations, I was definitely relieved when Ana suggested that we leave early, before general drunkenness took over. Not all of the Mexicans were hostile, of course, but those who were appeared to be serious about it, and I certainly didn't want any sharp steel between my ribs.

I might add here that had I been summoned into this crowd as a doctor I would have had little to fear. I've been in some mighty rough places as a doctor and never had any problems. Even when I stared into a pistol barrel at point-blank range, the gunman said, not unkindly, "Stay out of this, Doc."

As weeks passed, I was becoming very fond of Ana, an emotion that she seemed to share. Sensing my feelings, she stated, somewhat reluctantly, I thought, "It just wouldn't work out." And she bravely closed that chapter by moving to Pueblo, Colorado, putting a thousand miles between us. Except for the exchange of a few letters, Ana moved out of my life. I certainly wish her well.

Before Ana another dark-eyed beauty had gotten my attention. Her mother was Mexican and her father Italian. Like Longfellow's peregrinacious heroine from Acadia, her name was Evangeline, and she was assistant in the clinic pharmacy in the hospital basement. She was petite, smart, lovely, and altogether desirable.

Although I admired her greatly, it was from afar. I had never dated her or had much opportunity to be with her. She must have suspected my adoration, however, because one evening when she had a problem she came to me for help.

"I'm in trouble," she stated simply. My heart jumped. What could be her problem? She couldn't have been indiscreet.

"I've locked my keys in the pharmacy, and I have to open up in the morning. I don't want anyone to know I've pulled such a dumb trick. What can we do?" The "we" thrilled me, I'll admit, because any coupling with Evangeline was exciting.

"Let's take a look," I said, leading the way down to the now deserted clinic area. The pharmacy door was tightly closed, and the security of its big Yale lock defied all my amateurish attempts at lock-picking. The dispensing window had no glass but was protected instead by vertical iron bars. Cautiously I thrust my head through the bars far enough for my ears to complain of compression; then, backing out, I suggested to Evangeline, "As small as you are, I believe you could wiggle through."

She looked skeptical but climbed on a chair and thrust her head through the bars as far as the shoulders. "Fine!" I exclaimed. "I believe you can make it." I was thinking of obstetrics; once the baby's head is out, extraction of the body is assured.

Then I looked at her hips, full, rounded hips of a mature woman, and I had doubts. Just then she withdrew her head in near panic. "I'm afraid I'll get caught," she explained somewhat sheepishly, disappointed at not being able to follow through with my suggestion.

"I'll try again," I said. Being slender also, I believed that success was possible, but first I removed shirt, undershirt, and belt to avoid getting hung up. Evangeline turned her head as I peeled down. Modesty still existed in those days. ("In those high and far off times," as Kipling might say.)

Disregarding the complaints of my ears, I worked my head between the bars. Then twisting sideways I managed to get an arm through. Next came the other arm, and I was through to the waist. There I seemed to stick, half in, half out, trapped between bars. "Evangeline," I said. "You're going to have to unbutton my pants and pull 'em off."

"I couldn't do that!" she exclaimed, mortified.

"It's the only way. I can't stay hung up like this till someone comes. Get 'em off!"

So, blushing furiously, she unbuttoned my fly and slid my trousers off. I was hoping that my anxiety would offset the physiological reaction that might be expected through having this gorgeous, warm female creature so close, unbuttoning my fly. I did not need any further obstacles to passing my hips through the bars. Fortunately, I was able to wriggle on through, naked except for my shorts.

Quickly I opened the door for "my lady" to enter, but she did not. She turned her embarrassed face away and thrust my clothes in through the door. I quickly put them on, stepped out, and handed her the keys. I was hoping for a brief kiss of gratitude, but her only emotion now was embarrassment and perhaps actual shame—shame at removing a man's pants and seeing him nearly naked. The moral code of the upper-class Mexicans was strict, and she had surely fractured it. She thanked me and fled. A week went by before she felt brazen enough to speak to me again. She avoided me from that time on, unfair behavior that had me feeling sorry for myself.

San Antonio is a beautiful city, serene and lovely. What we saw at the Greene would tend to give a very wrong impression of the city as a whole. Most of its citizens were unaware of what went on at our beloved Bucket of Blood. Many may not even have known of its existence, although they couldn't miss hearing those Saturday night sirens.

Today on a different site a huge modern medical center reflects the progress made since our days at the Greene. Our old hospital has been refurbished as a limited facility, but the venerable Robert B. Greene Memorial Hospital of Bexar County and the city of San Antonio as we knew it is now a forgotten relic.

Eighteen

Sidney, Nebraska! I had once in college dated a girl from Sidney, my only knowledge of the place. I was now coming as an assistant to an established doctor who had promised me a salary of $175 a month—not much, even in 1937, but it would be dependable and would serve until something better could be found. I had to have some income right away. Besides, my employer did lots of surgery, and he promised to push me in surgery, although his efforts in that direction proved to be less than encouraging.

I was surprised to learn that the wet glove technique was still being used in surgery, since it had been pretty generally discarded elsewhere in favor of dry talcum powder. Gloves are worn, of course, to minimize infection. In earlier times they were soaked in a weak solution of phenol (carbolic acid), then drawn on wet over hands that had been steeped in the same stuff. Prolonged use of phenol in this manner caused constriction of the blood vessels in the hands to the point that some surgeons developed numbness and eventually gangrene of the fingers, resulting in amputation. Learning of this hazard, our chief here in Sidney had switched to soapsuds by the time I came on the scene. Soap is preferable to phenol, but compared to powder, the cold, clammy, wet suds felt like a miserable step backward.

Our chief was an aggressive surgeon, having performed successfully some pretty innovative procedures for a small rural hospital, a private hospital that he had built and owned. Just before my arrival, he had been called out in the country to see a young lad who had been kicked in the head by a horse. The boy had an open, depressed skull fracture. Lest delay be fatal, the doctor had done some preliminary work right there in the barn, using tweezers to pluck out small fragments of bone, hair, and bits of damaged brain tissue before moving the boy to the hospital. The boy recovered. Sometime later, however, one of his acquaintances made the remark, "Doc must have overlooked a few bits of manure. The kid gets some pretty shitty ideas now and then."

Although the old doctor was the most capable surgeon in the area, he was difficult to work with because he believed that no one could be trusted. Being always under suspicious scrutiny made me so uncomfortable that I finally asked, "Doctor, don't you ever trust anyone?"

His answer was revealing: "I wouldn't trust my own mother."

In fairness to the man, I should state that he was experiencing discomfort from heart trouble, a condition that would not inject much hilarity into his disposition. He had probably experienced his best years before my arrival. I have referred to him as the "old doctor," although in years he was only in his late fifties.

There were other doctors in town, all trying to provide good service. Two doctor brothers, however, became enamored briefly with an Abrams diagnostic machine, a creation that had aroused a good deal of public interest, appearing, as it did, at a time when so many newly conceived scientific gadgets were being adopted. I do not know whether the brothers believed in it. Had it really worked, it would have been a marvelous boon.

On the Abrams machine the patient was hooked up to wires or electrodes, and when the "juice" was turned on he was treated to an impressive display of flashing lights, whirring and buzzing sounds, and a tingling sensation that gave him the impression that he was being intimately evaluated by mysterious intricacies deep within the machine. Then, after a suspenseful interval of wise evaluation, the machine would come up with a diagnosis, I believe a number indexed to a chart. I do not know whether the diagnosis was the result of random selection or whether the operator had a secret means of influencing the decision. He would have to apprise the machine out of the general area being studied so it would not, for example, diagnose gout as pneumonia.

'Ere long the brothers realized that ethics prohibited use of the fraudulent contraption, and they discarded it. Later, after one of the brothers died, the survivor still employed unusual tactics. In struggling with diagnosis and treatment, he consulted with his brother, who could now be reached only through a spiritualistic seance. As the number of people who believed in spiritual consultation was limited, the surviving doctor's patient load diminished considerably, which he may have secretly welcomed as he was getting old and tired. In fact, before long he moved on to where he presumably could contact his brother more directly.

About this time, I was summoned as a medical witness in a court case. A damage suit was in progress over an auto accident. I was intrigued by the informality of the scene, which seemed to emphasize the casual atmosphere of the time.

The attorney for the plaintiff, chomping on the end of a dead cigar, sat huddled with his little group on one side of the courtroom, while his opponent, counsel for the defense, sat with his smaller group on the other side. The defense attorney was chewing a generous quid of tobacco so that he would be ready with an adequate charge of tobacco juice whenever someone made a statement that was not to his liking. When this happened, and it seemed to occur frequently, he would grunt his disapproval and spout a frighteningly large bolus of disgusting brown liquid in the direction of one of the courtroom's numerous brass spittoons. Surprisingly, the man never missed. But I felt compassion for the people who cleaned up the place during the years when he was developing his phenomenal skill. The subsequent disappearance of spittoons has been a great step forward, and we are assured by tobacco advertisers that the large quid can now be replaced by "a little pinch between your cheek and gums" (a nasty place to develop cancer).

The judge seemed benignly indifferent to all the chewing and spitting. The spitting expert won. Case closed.

Nineteen

I was disappointed with the degree of stress that seemed to permeate our hospital. I would stay a year, as promised. Then I would depart this arena of tension, and disappear. But with the approach of year's end, things changed abruptly. My employer died.

If I stayed on, I would no longer be an employee. I would be boss, the new chief. Why not give it a whirl? From his widow I purchased all the equipment and leased the hospital. "With what?" you may well ask.

The widow was eager to be out of the hospital business, and she was kind enough to offer terms that I felt I could handle. True, it would be a big headache, but it would be mine to deal with in my own way. No more energy wasted in trying to avoid my employer's wrath. I could now mold our little twenty-bed hospital staff into an efficient, caring team held together by an espirit de corps that would banish fear and stress. We could relax and do our jobs. Our credo would be simple and direct, the same as that of my predecessor: "At all times do what is best for the patient." That was the standard by which we lived and worked, but we tried to achieve it with less stress.

In defusing the tension among the staff I was rewarded by a perfusion of cheerfulness into the general atmosphere. People were smiling more. They acted as if they enjoyed coming to work. And this cheerfulness was psychologically beneficial to the patients. In dispelling gloom it fostered recovery.

Among the treasures I had purchased was a nearly antique examining table. Actually it was an ingeniously contrived chair-table combination, a comfortable chair when upright and an examining table when extended out flat. The back could be raised and lowered, as could the knees and feet. It also sported a fancy movable headrest and several puzzling control levers.

You had to be careful which of the control levers was pulled. One tipped the table top sharply to the side to facilitate sliding a patient off onto a stretcher—or onto the floor, as I discovered while learning the controls, a maneuver that tended to undermine the patient's confidence.

Another trick this chair-table played on me was the result of my not noticing that its base was much longer in one direction than the other. The longer diameter was supposed to parallel the extended table to give stability when it was converted into the chair configuration.

A frail old woman was in the chair, and when she attempted to leave, she stood up on the step of the chair before stepping onto the floor. But the chair, being on a free swivel, had turned crosswise on its base. Thus when she put her weight on the step, the chair tipped forward, spilling her onto the floor. To top it off in grand style, as the chair fell completely over, the headrest arced downward and clobbered her on top of the head.

My heart was in my mouth. I had been on my own for only a few days. What a way to attract patients! My effusive apologies as I rescued the old woman seemed to fall on deaf ears. She was grim. She fled the office without a word and never returned, leaving me apprehensively trying to contrive a legal defense. The defense was never needed. She simply disappeared.

One of the more exciting features of my newly acquired hospital was the elevator. It was a hand-fired rig, operated by pulling a rope like a block and tackle. It had counterweights that were estimated to balance the weight of an average load, thus lessening the amount of pull required on the rope when going up. A hand brake on the cable could be locked at each floor. We had to impress on all personnel the importance of setting the brake, especially at the lower levels. If the brake was not locked, and if there was no load on the elevator, it would, in a sudden rush of freedom, rumble rapidly upward to crash against the top of the shaft—an impact that would scare hell out of everyone within earshot. There was an automatic brake that would lock in case the supporting cables gave way, but that only prevented the cage from falling. It was quite indifferent to a runaway cage going upward.

One day an attendant, wheeling a patient off the elevator, failed to lock the brake. She stepped off the elevator platform and turned to pull the wheeled stretcher off feet first. It was well that the patient was not strapped down. Before the attendant could pull the stretcher clear, the elevator started upward. The two wheels at the head of the cart were still on the elevator platform and going up. This action quickly tipped the stretcher at such a steep angle that the patient slid off onto the floor while the stretcher, with the two wheels still on the platform, was carried up to where it jammed at the top of the elevator door, stopping the elevator and almost stopping the heart of the attendant. It was never again necessary to caution her to set the brake.

We boasted two x-ray machines, a big Kelley-Koett at the doctor's office and a smaller "portable" Victor at the hospital that could be wheeled into patients' rooms. Both were manufactured before shockproof machines were available. Both had exposed high-voltage wires that dared any terrified amateur to get too close.

During the days when my former chief was still alive, a local doctor who had no x-ray brought in a boy with a broken arm. He wanted pictures without delay, but our chief was out for a bit, and no one else was allowed to touch the machines. Bristling with impatience, Dr. A. "allowed" that he would take the x-rays. "Oh, no!" pleaded the head nurse. "No one is supposed to touch the machine."

"We'll see about that," replied Dr. A. grimly. He was understandably upset over the delay. He strode up to the machine, glanced at the dials, and threw the main switch. The tube was thus activated and ready to go. He then followed correct procedure by placing a film cassette under the injured arm and setting the timer. But he was too close to the wires. When he hit the timer, sparks flew, and the doctor hit the floor unconscious.

Enter here the chief. With no apparent concern for the body on the floor, he stepped over him and shut off the machine. No one else was hurt. A nurse, bending solicitously over the injured doctor, queried anxiously, "Aren't you going to help him?"

"Serves him right," was the callous reply. "He's not supposed to meddle with the x-ray."

By this time the shock victim was stirring. If the jolt had momentarily stopped his heart, the effect had soon worn off, as he was now able to sit up. Demoralized, he turned the fracture case over to our chief and departed.

The machine in the doctor's office downtown, the big Kelley, had a huge rotating rectifier. It had open wires strung across the room over the x-ray table so that the large Coolidge tube could be rolled back and forth for positioning over different areas. There was no dial on which to read the voltage setting. Voltage was determined by the spark gap method, a procedure that used the fact that under "normal" conditions a spark will jump about one centimeter for each thousand volts difference in potential between two large brass balls. Thus for fifty KV (50,000 volts), the spark would arc across fifty centimeters, nearly twenty inches. The balls would be adjusted to the appropriate setting or separation and the machine "revved up" until sparking occurred.

The sudden loud crackle and the arcing blue lightning so close at hand could be counted on to create bug-eyed anxiety in most patients, even though they were warned beforehand. Modern shockproof machines have no such flamboyant character or personality. They have to be concerned with safety.

In those colorful days we were, through ignorance, much less concerned about the possible ill effects of radiation. We didn't always bother with lead aprons or gloves. Of course, lead gloves are impractical when you're probing under the fluoroscopic screen for a foreign body. We commonly used the fluoroscope for that purpose and occasionally for setting bones. And the level of voltage for fluoroscopy is low, permitting the body to absorb more of the radiation. (Higher voltage drives the rays through and out.)

I was foolish enough to sit in the same room with the patient when giving x-ray therapy with the big Kelley-Koett. I had to hold down the button switch. Before long, however, I quit using the machine for therapy. I knew the exposure required to produce erythema (like a sunburn), but I was not sure of my Roentgen units, the measurements of exposure the specialists were beginning to use.

Before quitting, however, I was lucky enough to bring about the remission of large, intra-abdominal lymphomatous tumors in an old woman who was terrified of surgery. She died of other causes two years later, still in remission; hence we had obviously done her a favor.

I did less well on myself. For fifteen years I was mildly distressed by an eczema-like irritation of my hands from x-ray burns. Over several years I had carelessly exposed myself to probably twenty times the supposed maximum total safe level for a lifetime, and although there is still time for me to develop cancer, I'm pleased to note that I don't glow in the dark or fog Kodak film.

Besides our own x-ray work I also took all the dental films for Dr. Pettibone, a very competent dentist with offices across the hall. One day I was in his chair as a patient while he was fitting an inlay. "How long," I asked, "can I expect this inlay to last?"

"Well," he began cautiously, "I put one in for a man six weeks ago that I know will last at least fifty years."

"How can you be sure of that?"

"He just died!"

Twenty

Within a year I realized that I needed help. I was able to lure to Sidney a very competent young doctor named Chris Bitner, who was so youthful that many people thought he was an intern. A few years later another valuable man, Dr. James Thayer, joined our staff, and for nearly fifty years we worked amicably together, a lengthy solidarity that is unusual among doctors, who tend to be vigorously individualistic.

Rural medical practice provides many interesting sidelights. I encountered some such one night when called to attend a woman in labor. She lived with Lizzie, her married sister, in a shack of forbidding squalor. I don't expect you to believe this, but there were two pet chickens roosting on the head of the old iron bed. I don't know whether they were trained to poop away from the bed, although I'll concede that they were aimed away from the bed as I entered. I assumed that the man present was the husband of the woman in labor. No, he was Lizzie's husband. But he was the father of the baby. I must have looked puzzled as he explained the situation: "You see, we have just the one bed where we all sleep. And," he added a bit sheepishly, I thought, "we don't have electric lights." In other words, any port in a storm or in the dark.

Another obstetric call came during a cold winter night. I grabbed my "out bag," picked up a nurse, and drove as fast as the snow would permit several miles out into the country. We waded through snow to a dugout house, mostly underground. The single kerosene lamp faintly disclosed a young woman lying in an old iron bed under blankets and soogans (comforters). Edna, my nurse, pulled back the covers so that we could at least see the patient. She was wearing her husband's heavy winter underwear that had a strangely bulging crotch. As we watched, the bulge moved. I hastened to expose the field by unbuttoning the drop seat of the underwear, disclosing not only the baby but also the afterbirth, all in a mass of blood, bowel movement, goo, and clots. Edna, the nurse, turned green. It was one of the few times she almost fainted on me.

But, she rallied and was able to clean up the baby while I tried to gather up the mess around the mother with newspapers. The grandmother was waiting to receive the baby, having just stoked the little monkey stove with a double handful of slack coal. She smacked her hands together to shake off some of the coal dust and accepted the baby.

That made three children for this family. The father was standing by looking indifferent. Even the need for keeping the stove going was a concept he had not yet assimilated. He seemed pretty laid back, as was evidenced by his not wanting to be bothered with making the drive to town for a marriage license, but in his defense I should explain that the roads out that way were pretty bad.

A more difficult OB came my way about 1940. I delivered this woman at home, a mistake I would not make now. It was her first baby, an exceedingly tough delivery, mid-forceps and a big episiotomy. An episiotomy is a slicing cut that enlarges the vaginal opening. The anesthetist needed my constant supervision because he was dripping chloroform, and he had never seen a chloroform bottle before. He was the patient's husband. When we finally got the baby out, we could see why delivery had been so difficult. The baby weighed just under twelve pounds.

Mother and baby did well, but the father was upset at my high fee—$45. He knew the going rate was $35. But he agreed that the fee was not exorbitant when I explained that the $35 fee was for an uncomplicated case. He realized that her case could not be casually passed off as uncomplicated.

The grandmother of a much smaller infant was disappointed that her new grandchild weighed only three and one-half pounds. "My God," she exclaimed. "I've fried chickens bigger than that!"

More OB: "We've got a lady out here that's bleeding real bad!" Dr. Thayer was greeted with this message when he answered an early morning phone call. "Get her in to the hospital right away," he advised.

"We can't. She's got chills and fever too. She's too sick to come to the hospital."

"What the devil do you think hospitals are for? Get her in!"

It turned out to be one of those cases that you pray will go somewhere else. The woman was eight months pregnant, and she was certainly hemorrhaging. She was uremic from toxic nephrosis (kidney failure). Her blood pressure was dangerously high. She had a temperature of 105 from a pneumonia that was superimposed on tuberculosis. As soon as we got her to bed, she went into convulsions. She was indeed too sick to be anywhere except the morgue.

After supportive treatment, she seemed somewhat improved. Unfortunately, she was conscious. I say unfortunately because she was as mean and ungrateful a wretch as could be imagined, screaming curses and obscenities at the nurses who were trying to help her.

At one point a nurse heard a very loud thump in this patient's room. "My God, she's fallen out of bed." (We'll call her "Manny.")

Sure enough! As the nurse reached the room Manny was climbing back into bed. The nurse rushed to give assistance but was vigorously repulsed. "Git outta the way," screamed Manny angrily. "These God-damned doctors don't know nothin'. I'm gonna bring this baby!" Whereupon, to the nurse's amazement and horror, she stood up in bed, jumped out, and landed flat-footed on the floor.

As would be expected, she restarted the hemorrhage. Now we did have a dilemma. She had a placenta previa, meaning the placenta was plastered over the inner opening of the cervical canal. If we let her go into labor, mother and baby both would be expected to bleed to death. She was still toxic from the nephrosis, still had her tuberculous pneumonia with high fever, and high blood pressure, and the bleeding was alarming.

Why not section her? Why indeed? Caesarean operation would probably save the baby but perhaps kill the mother, yet delaying would increase the risk to both. We couldn't seem to match her blood.

When is the best time to jump off a moving train? Wait till it slows or stops, of course. But suppose it's accelerating all the time, faster, faster, and you have to get off. Then what? We opted for immediate surgery. This proved to be a satisfactory decision. With constant, continuous follow-up care by our dedicated staff, mother and baby both survived.

After ten days the mother was referred to the state hospital for the tuberculous. We never heard whether she went. I doubt that she did. It would just have meant more "God-damned doctors."

Twenty-one

During my first year in Sidney I was summoned one cold winter night to attend a woman out in the country who was suffering severe abdominal pain. She was badly distended, a condition that had developed after she had eaten popcorn. How much popcorn? "Three dishpans full" (and with no teeth for chewing). She was subject to constipation anyway, and this gluttonous stuffing of the gut had apparently overwhelmed her peristalsis (intestinal activity).

She was moaning and groaning and rolling all over the bed. She needed a powerful carminative (gas mover). I always liked the sound of that word, yet a carminative here would be about as effective as sending Tom Thumb out to slay a dinosaur with a pocket knife.

She needed an enema, probably repeated enemas, yet she balked at hospitalization, and I was too inexperienced and too accommodating to assert myself. "But you'll need enemas," I advised.

"We can do that here," she countered. "Pa, where's the injection outfit?"

At that time everything that could possibly be treated at home was attempted there first, and of course I wished to please these people if possible. Pa produced the hot water bottle and tubing all right, but he handed them to me. He wanted no part in the operation, a complication that surprised and distressed me. I was not accustomed to giving enemas either.

The urgency of the situation, however, overrode my prudish revulsion. I filled the bag with warm water and approached the bed and the biggest bare bottom I had ever seen. The patient lay on her side, flannel nighty hiked up to her waist. With one hand she held the buttock on that side pried upward, effectively exposing the brazen bulls-eye, which I could scarcely miss even in the subdued light of the single coal oil lamp.

With the well-greased rectal tip inserted, I asked her to hold it in place. "I can't reach it," she said, and obesity did render her cooperation difficult. So I had to keep the plug in the dike myself.

I raised the bag.

Almost at once her groaning increased, and she tried to resume her rolling on the bed. To keep the rectal tip in place I found myself rolling back and forth with her. Once as she rolled on her back, she kicked me in the head, but I held fast. Presently she cried out, "I can go now. I can go. Let me up!"

I was only too glad to comply, but she was quicker. Despite her bulk, she leaped from the bed before I could clamp the tube, and the freed nozzle squirted water in my face and all over the bed while I was scrambling to get the thunder bucket shoved under her in preparation for the expected explosion.

Her supreme lack of embarrassment did much to allay my own discomfort as one thunderous blast after another reverberated in the bucket. Gratified (and wet), I started from the room with the equipment. "Wait; there's more!" she cried. "We'll have to go another round."

And indeed we did. In fact we went two more rounds. I was getting pretty good at rolling with her on the bed—hardly what one usually envisions at the mention of a roll in bed. We eventually got her deflated and fairly comfortable.

Looking back on the experience, I feel a little foolish at letting myself get roped in on such an event, but I make no apology for our wrestling match because the patient benefited from it.

In speaking of enemas for the relief of gas, I'd like to quote a doctor who ordered a hot milk and molasses enema for this purpose. The nurse, never having heard of this old-fashioned mixture, asked questioningly if it would really be effective. "Well," he replied, "we'll put it this way: if the patient happens to be eating a sandwich at the time, it'll suck it right out of his hand."

Twenty-two

Sidney in the thirties was an average farmer-oriented Saturday
night town. Paving of some of the streets was in progress. We killed
a rattlesnake in front of the hospital. Snakes were a frequent hazard
on the golf course. A man from the produce house chased an escaped chicken through the downtown area at a mad run. I was
cheering for the chicken, literally running for its life, but we lost.

I missed out on the last big gun battle in town by reason of being
in Moose, Wyoming, getting married. The shoot-out was between
bank robbers and local police (and citizens) and took place right in
front of my office. As I recall, two of the bad guys were appre-
hended after being wounded, and one was killed.

On learning that I had missed the action while getting married,
one of my friends commented, "Your battles will come later." But
we never had a battle of consequence, probably because my wife
was a saint.

We did retain for several more years our little down-home
whorehouse, with a cat walk that communicated with the second
story of the Commercial Hotel. Drummers (traveling salesmen
who drummed up business for their companies) preferred this dis-
creet access. The house was run by a relatively young madam who
had come up from the ranks. She was one of the heart-of-gold pioneer type (some of this type did really exist outside of western lit-
erature). Old men, sick or down on their luck, were permitted to

rent rooms she was not using, whether they could pay or not. She often fed them free, too, and gave them nursing care when needed.

Sometimes she would call me and perhaps say, "I've got an old boy in Number Eleven who's pretty sick. I gave him an enema last night, but he's still awfully weak. Do you suppose you could look at him?"

How could I refuse? Her Florence Nightingale activities were compassionately given gratis. Why not mine? I would go—and perhaps accidentally leave my hat, as I did a few times before I quit wearing one. This would upset Edna, my office nurse, because one of the girls would bring it back during office hours, with some comment about my having left it. "It even has your name in it," she reminded me.

Occasionally we were treated to colorful home remedies, the flagship of these being, perhaps, the cow-manure poultice. Fresh cow manure was spread generously like a thick layer of peanut butter over a large piece of flannel, which was then slapped onto the chest goo-down next to the skin to treat chest colds or pneumonia. Or the same remedy might be applied over a joint for relief of rheumatism. Additional layers of flannel were usually added to hold in the heat and retard evaporation and leakage. Surprisingly, this treatment was as effective as a mustard plaster or any of the commercially available chest rubs, possibly more so. And it was cheap. Enzymes and secretions in the manure are efficient rubifacients—they irritate the skin, thus drawing blood to the area as effectively as a hot pack. And the manure poultice does not need the constant attention required by a hot pack. Yet even after the obvious advantages were pointed out to our nurses, they still preferred a different approach. I suppose there's no accounting for taste—or smell.

In hearing of the cow-manure poultice, some skeptics seem to doubt that it was actually used. I can assure you that it was. I remember one old woman with an arthritic ankle who required help getting into the office because she kept her bad foot immersed in a big bucket of fresh cow manure. She acted as though this were nothing unusual. Her son, however, was obviously embarrassed as he was obliged to walk bent over, clinging to the bail of the bucket and endeavoring to synchronize his movements to accommodate her awkward, clumping gait. Their entrance command center stage in our reception room. I was fascinated. Could she not bear to be separated from her therapeutic goop long enough to walk in from the car without it? If the stuff were that effective, why consult a doctor?

Cleansing of the foot and ankle were facilitated by repeated rinsing and flushing in the toilet bowl, and it revealed skin that was overirritated, almost blistered, for which we applied a soothing dressing. I advised that since the maximum benefits of the dip had now been realized, we could switch to internal medication. I felt sure that her dedication to the bovine slop would not include taking it internally so I prescribed something of a more conventional nature, and we emptied the bucket in the toilet, at the risk of developing within the toilet a taste for something we could not ordinarily provide.

With the cane that we provided, and no bucket, the patient's gait improved perceptibly. The son fled with the bucket, glad to escape the scowling disapproval of the people in our waiting room.

Twenty-three

Our hospital was a two-and-one-half story building. Behind it was a concrete parking area. At one time we had a pneumonia patient in a top-floor room overlooking this parking area. He was sick enough to require a special nurse.

In the middle of a cold winter night I got a frantic call that this patient was missing! How in the name of everything reasonable could he possibly be missing? During the very few minutes that it took his nurse to go for fresh drinking water, he had raised the window and jumped out, taking the screen with him. But they could not find him!

I practically leaped from the bed into my clothes, endeavoring to frame words of condolence to the family and wondering what legal action I might be facing. Where in hell could the patient be? And how could he even survive the two-and-one-half-story drop onto concrete? It was about twelve degrees Fahrenheit, and this guy out there in nothing but a hospital gown—and with pneumonia and high fever, plus the broken bones from the fall! It raised terrifying thoughts as we searched the surrounding grounds.

Finally, my flashlight picked out something white under a clump of bushes, his hospital gown. He was hunched in there hiding. I could not believe his lack of injuries: no broken bones, only minor bruises and abrasions. Nothing noticeable enough to cause the family to ask questions. Incredible!

In recalling his sensationally wild leap I can scarcely say that his recovery from the pneumonia was uneventful, but is was, thank God, successful. Every time I look up at that window, I am amazed anew. Delirium assuredly can cause strange behavior.

It is not always easy to determine whether a patient is lucid. I did feel, however, that one of our hospital patients was confused when he strode boldly into a woman's room wearing absolutely nothing but a large black cowboy hat. Her immediate fright was considerably mollified when he asked casually if she knew the location of the bathroom. Later she thought the incident hilarious, stating that it would make her hospital stay something to remember. The man, being confused, had no recollection of his strikingly bold behavior.

Sometimes delirium is obvious, sometimes not. In answering a call bell one of our nurses was surprised by the patient's comment, "Was that naked lady who just went by my door supposed to leave? I think she went outside." Now, was this delirium speaking, or was the naked lady real and she the one confused? The nurse wisely rushed outside to take a look.

Sure enough, there was the naked lady, already half a block away and making good time. A spirited foot race ensued, much to the amazement of chance onlookers.

After finally capturing the fugitive, the nurse regretted not having brought along some type of cover. Her discomfort is understandable when you visualize her three-block walk back to the hospital, arm in arm with a naked woman.

Delirium in an otherwise healthy person usually results from a dangerous buildup of toxins, most frequently from infection. Another "nudist" fled the hospital one cold night and flagged down a car. The motorist was so astonished that he stopped and drove the man home as requested.

Since the patient's wife knew that he was critically ill with peritonitis, she was stunned by his unexpected arrival—naked and all that. The patient justified his action by saying, "The hospital was OK while Dr. Cook was in charge, but when that drunken army major took over things sure went to hell." His subsequent recovery back in the hospital seemed colorless by comparison. People who seem sensible enough to get by in most everyday situations are often closer to the ragged edge than we realize. We had one such man in the hospital following the bite of a "mad" dog. His antics were almost entertaining. He was unaware that the incubation period of rabies is several weeks and he developed very unusual symptoms in a few hours, symptoms that were the result of self-hypnosis and a vivid imagination, combined with fear of rabies and ignorance of its actual symptoms.

As I came down the hospital corridor, I could hear him barking like a dog. The nurses warned me about entering his room. He had already bitten one of them, fortunately not severely.

As I cracked the door and peered in, he crouched on all fours, then leaped for the door, growling and snarling. To avoid a physical encounter I hastily backed off and closed the door, hoping he would tire of this circus-like performance. Oddly enough, he seemed in genuine panic.

Soon I tried again, this time speaking through the closed door. "Jerry," I said, "you'd better let me give you an antidote before you get any weaker." No response. "Jerry," I said again, "we don't want you to die on our hands. I'm coming in to give you the antidote."

I opened the door, surprised to see him sitting wide-eyed on the edge of the bed, quiet but still frightened. "We'll get this shot into you before the fits come back," I added in reassuring tones. After receiving the sedative, Jerry lapsed into peaceful slumber. Next day he was released, "cured," to return to his job of repairing streets. To my knowledge, he has had no further psychotic behavior.

As is often the case, the many fine people in our area might be considered less newsworthy than the occasional oddball such as the middle-aged woman who apparently became tired of her husband. He was brought in one evening with severe bruises of his legs.

"My wife did this to me," he explained. "I was in the garage when she drove in. She pinned me against the end of the garage, even broke out part of the wall!"

"What an unfortunate accident!" I sympathized.

"It was no accident," he wailed. "She's tryin' to kill me. She tried first with a butcher knife, then with poison; she set me on fire; and now this. I'm beginning to be afraid of that woman." Really!

I knew what he meant because I was aware that she was psychotic. Later she was confined in a mental institution. Some discerning wag years ago made this catchy statement: "The neurotic builds castles in the air. The schizophrenic lives in them, and the psychiatrist goes around collecting the rent."

One Sunday morning I was so sleepy that Ruth answered the phone for me. I heard her say, "I believe you have the wrong number." But the person on the line kept talking, and Ruth handed the phone to me saying, "They want the key to the handcuffs."

Immediately my mind reverted to the previous night's events at the hospital. We were so crowded that a woman in labor had to be placed on a cot in the hall. I was working late in the evening on records and correspondence in our clinic office, which we had recently moved from downtown into the hospital building.

For some reason I was experiencing a strange feeling of impending disaster that was suddenly augmented by the sound of running feet descending the stairs. The charge nurse burst in on me in near panic. "The man in Room 9 is dragging your OB off the cot!"

The man in Room 9 was a hemorrhoidectomy patient who was to have been released, but he had that afternoon developed delirium tremens. We had not known that he was a boozer, and of course he had not mentioned it.

I raced up the stairs in time to hear him shout savagely, "Get your ass in here in bed where you belong!" In the confusion of the delirium tremens he thought she was his wife. She was terrified. This was not what she had expected in the hospital.

The man, a rough-looking truck driver, was not about to relinquish his claim on the frightened woman, who found herself the center of a tug-of-war as I endeavored to pull her away from him. Infuriated, he took a powerful swing at me with his fist. I ducked, thinking, "I'm going to have to hit him." Yet I hesitated, as visions of newspaper headlines raced through my mind: DR. COOK SLUGS PATIENT IN HOSPITAL.

After his next swing I slipped in and quickly grabbed him by the throat, shutting off his carotid arteries with thumb pressure. Before he could comprehend what was happening, he slumped unconscious to the floor.

Calling for the nurse to bring a sedative shot, I picked him up off the floor, carried him back to Room 9, and threw him on the bed.

At my request, the nurse called the police for a pair of handcuffs, and with our man securely shackled to the bed frame I felt free to reassure the frightened woman. I sat on the edge of her cot for some time, telling her that she was now safe. "We've got him handcuffed to the bed, and the bed won't go through the door. He can't bother you anymore."

That was one time I was glad we had moved the clinic into the hospital building. There was another occasion when I was not so glad, since the open stairway conveyed sound upstairs like a megaphone. One of the girls working in the clinic was a luscious blond who looked like a sex goddess. She was joking with the last patient of the day, a middle-aged prankster who enjoyed teasing her. As he was leaving, he made an elaborate pass at her, and she, ready for any end-of-the-day hilarity, squealed and jumped into the hallway, laughing loudly.

With such an invitation to horseplay, our man gave chase. Before I could act, they were running up and down the long hallway with the girl shrieking at me to rescue her.

But that was definitely not the impression everyone upstairs was getting. Not once did she scream, "Dr. Cook, help me!" or "Stop him." Instead, she was yelling, "Oh, Dr. Cook. Oo-oo-ooh, Dr. Cook!" To anyone within earshot I was obviously attempting a vigorous seduction and meeting with diminishing resistance.

I heard unfavorable comments later. What the devil could I say? They *heard* what was going on, didn't they?

Twenty-four

Obstetrics is usually one of the more gratifying areas of medical practice. Birth is such a happy time when all goes well, as it usually does. The mother is delighted to have the baby outside at last where she can hold him or her in her arms. She is almost as happy over having lost the ponderous bulge that has been giving her increasing discomfort.

Often in the delivery room, when the young mother was relaxing after delivery, I would say, "Feel your stomach." She would start reaching for it in midair almost a foot in front of her now flattened abdomen. What a welcome change.

Although usually a delight, obstetrics can be as difficult and hazardous as any other field of medicine or surgery. The old cliché "From the ridiculous to the sublime" here reads "From essentially zero risk to fatality." I was extremely lucky in not drawing one of the fatalities, one of those rare cases that cannot be saved.

I'll mention some of the near zero risks. I recall especially three, whose labors I shall describe in their own words. One said, "I just felt a little tinkle down there, and the baby came out."

Another, who lived in Potter, twenty miles west, suddenly, with no previous mention of labor, shouted to her husband, "Call Dr. Sloan!"

"Why not Dr. Cook? He's your doctor."

"There's no time!" Dr. Sloan was the doctor in Potter who was trying to retire. "But while my husband was looking in the phone book for Dr. Sloan's number, the baby came out." No mention was made of pain or discomfort.

The third easy labor I found lying on the floor in the doorway between her kitchen and dining room. Even though I had dropped everything and raced to their home in response to her husband's frantic summons, I was not quick enough. There she lay with her baby, both crying. "Are you still having pain?" I asked sympathetically.

"No, no; I don't have any pain. I'm just thinking of what my friends will say. They'll think I'm an old cow. They'll say, 'That old cow couldn't even make it out of the barn.'"

At the opposite extreme are those brave young women who have a terrible struggle. Many died in pioneer days, in the west-bound wagon trains, for lack of skilled assistance. And many more babies succumbed.

I have been guilty occasionally of delivering a woman from below who should have had a caesarean. Normal delivery was the way to go. And the "test of labor" was often used as a criterion. The test of labor is merely the interval of time necessary to make a reasonable estimate as to whether a woman in labor can experience a normal delivery. There's nothing wrong with employing the test of labor providing one recognizes its impending failure before the woman is exhausted.

Sometimes a tiny splinter of a woman will bring forth an eight-pound baby with no trouble, while a large woman, whose birth canal seems more than ample, will become hung up in unsuccessful labor. X-rays and pelvic measurements and now ultrasound easily identify the cases that are sure to have trouble. The problem lies in identifying which women will deliver normally among those that are borderline.

I'll be glad when it becomes generally recognized that most cerebral palsy cases are probably not the result of birth injuries. We had one case, from an easy labor, that became moderately spastic, apparently from having excessive neonatal jaundice. The only other spastic baby born in our hospital that I'm aware of was born by

C-section to a woman who opted for the C-section *before* she went into labor. She wanted her tubes tied because she already had two badly spastic children. Birth injuries? Sounds like baloney! It's in the genes. (She had three spastic boys and three normal girls.)

My notes on the delivery of Lois C., a perfectly wonderful young woman, illustrate the problems encountered in a borderline case. My notes read: "Pelvis seems flat. Very difficult mid forceps. Big episiotomy and repair. Patient *good* throughout. Baby OK, but for heaven's sake section this girl next time!"

A healthy, cooperative farm girl was having a difficult delivery. Her observations of calf-pulling on the farm colored her comments, especially when she was half under anesthesia. After enduring some severe contractions, she was becoming a bit frantic. She realized that my pulling with forceps, though helpful, still made for slow progress. She came up with helpful suggestions: "Put a chain around that baby's neck, and pull. Hook on the truck and pull harder!" After a bit she advised, "It's not working. Get the tractor!"

Actually we did not have to resort to either of these unparalleled suggestions. We soon had a fine healthy baby without even warming up a golf cart.

To avoid the unforgivable catastrophe of mixing identities, we were careful to get the mother's thumbprint and her baby's footprints on the chart before the infant was taken from the delivery room. I recall asking the nurse, after a rather difficult delivery, "Did you get the baby's footprints?"

"Footprints!" exclaimed the mother, rousing partially from light anesthesia. "Don't try to tell me that child walked out of there!"

In addition to that woman I called "Manny," there was another OB who caused me extreme anxiety because of her poor health. Unlike "Manny" she was a sweet girl and had been a severe diabetic most of her life. I had seen her many times during her childhood with severe abdominal pains simulating appendicitis but actually brought on by impending diabetic coma. Later, as a young adult she developed multiple sclerosis, high blood pressure, and diabetic nephrosis (kidney poisoning). She married and experienced four successive pregnancies, each of which terminated in miscarriage.

Then, under limited supervision, she was able to carry one a bit longer, even felt life. But the "quickening" stopped. X-rays disclosed overlapping skull bones, a sure sign of fetal death, so labor was induced and she brought fourth a three-pound preemie—dead, of course.

In her sixth pregnancy she was more cooperative about prenatal care and more careful in controlling her diabetes. At eight months she was still feeling movement, but her blood pressure was very high, and she had marked swelling from the nephrosis. I explained the dangers of further delay, dangers to both her and the baby, and I urged immediate C-section to prevent another intrauterine death. She agreed, and both mother and baby survived, thank God.

She had refused tubal ligation, so in three years she was back, pregnant again. Of course, the same hazardous complications set in, aggravated by repetition. We sectioned her five weeks early. Again the baby lived, and again she refused tubal ligation. I should have done it anyway. Perhaps secretly she would have felt relieved of anxiety. But I don't like to play God, so I acceded to her instructions.

Five years went by before her next pregnancy. This time she was really sick. She couldn't walk because of the MS. She was in a wheelchair. Her diabetic nephrosis was grievously aggravated; her blood pressure dangerously high; she had visual disturbances and massive swelling. She should have been aborted. When she had five weeks to go, I said, "This is it! We must not wait any longer to operate."

"Remember, Doctor, I've become a Jehovah's Witness. I can't be transfused."

This was the last straw. I'd been sweating with anxiety ever since she had said she was pregnant, and now I was expected to operate with one hand tied behind my back. I said, "You mean if it's life or death, you'd rather die than take blood?"

"That's right," she replied, and her husband vigorously nodded his agreement, rather belligerently I thought, lest I challenge their beliefs.

"I'll tell you something," I said firmly. "If I hadn't taken care of you since you were a small child, I'd tell you to take your problems and go far away and never come back. But for you I'll do this just this one more time." I wanted to say, "Have your minister take care of you next time." But I didn't.

We operated six weeks before her due date and got a live baby. I was spared another confrontation. A year later, the mother died.

Not long after our struggle with this unfortunate diabetic mother, we had another brush with the Jehovah's Witness sect. A man was brought in with a bullet wound in the abdomen. He was bleeding internally so we made hasty preparations for blood matching and exploratory surgery. The anesthetist was quickly arranging his gear while Dr. Bitner and I were nearby scrubbing for surgery.

Just then our hospital administrator came rushing up. "Do you realize you've got a Jehovah's Witness here? He can't take that blood! What are are you going to do about it?"

Remembering the sick people I had abruptly deserted to cover this emergency, I'm afraid I let my disgust break through. "Hell, let him die if he wants to. It's his life."

The patient heard my comment, as I thought he might. He looked up apprehensively at the anesthetist and said weakly, "I'm really not one yet. I'm just studying to be one. If I need the blood, give it to me."

Score one for reason. He got the much-needed blood and survived. I have no quarrel with what people want to believe, but when these folks quote the Bible as their authority for not taking blood, I wonder who, in biblical times, was contemplating a transfusion. People can believe or do what they wish *except* when it affects the outcome of my surgery.

Twenty-five

A local doctor noticed one of his patients driving in a most erratic manner. Fearing that the driver was apt to have an accident, he followed. Sure enough, as the car rounded a corner onto Toledo Street, the driver failed to straighten out the wheel. The car jumped the curb and crashed into a tree.

The doctor hurried to the scene, hoping the driver was not injured. He was not, but he did seem quite inebriated. "Harry, are you drunk?" demanded the doctor accusingly.

"Hell, yes!" was Harry's sluggish reply. "Do yuh think I'm a stunt driver?"

I was terribly frightened one time by a procedure that backfired. I was using the gravity method to collect blood for transfusion. The donor lay on the table. The needle in his vein was connected by a rubber tube to the collecting flask on the floor. A hollow needle had been thrust through the flask's stopper as an escape vent for the air that would be forced out to compensate for the volume of blood that was collecting in the flask.

When perhaps half the desired volume of blood had been drawn from the donor, the flow stopped. The venting needle had become plugged by a splash of blood. Without realizing that I should analyze how the laws of physics might affect the situation, I picked up the flask. This was a mistake. After the vent had become unplugged, blood continued to flow until the air pressure being built up in the flask equaled the weight of the blood in the descending tube. Then it stopped.

When I picked up the flask, the blood in the tube ran back into the donor. No problem at first. But then it was followed by a rush of air from within the top of the flask—air pressure that had built up since the plugging of the vent.

This injected air was carried to the heart through the venous system and promptly delivered to the lungs, where it caused an irritative cough that lasted for about five minutes. The cough was apparently the only ill effect.

I was acutely concerned, but I should have been terrified had I believed what we were taught in school, that a bubble of air injected intravenously is apt to be fatal. My skepticism concerning this theory was the result of two events that I had witnessed.

The first occurred in dog surgery. We had performed several surgical procedures on an anesthetized dog, a combination from which recovery was impossible. A painless death for the animal was indicated so I injected 20 cc of air directly into a vein, expecting the animal's immediate demise. Nothing happened. Another 20 cc. Still nothing. We had to use an overdose of anesthetic.

The second incident was more dramatic and even more convincing. A young doctor was donating blood in a large hospital where I happened to be working (not the Greene). In this case, I was only an observer. He was hooked up in the manner I described previously except that a suction pump was being used to extract the blood more quickly. Soon after the pump was turned on, the donor raised his head apprehensively and said, "I think I'm getting that air!" Then he passed out.

Sure enough. Investigation revealed that the suction tube had been connected to the pressure side of the pump. Considering how briskly the pump was whirring away, I can't see how he could have received less than a quart of air directly into the vein, and it may have been more. The doctor in charge clapped a stethoscope over the chest to check on heart action and apparently heard strange sounds. He said that instead of the usual "lupp-dupp," he heard "swish-swish," and he wondered if anyone else had ever heard air passing through a human heart.

The donor was unconscious for twenty to thirty minutes but was kept under observation for three days. Although experiencing weakness for nearly two months, he seemed eventually to recover without ill effects.

It is true that enough air can inactivate a vital part of the brain and possibly the heart by preventing necessary blood flow to those areas. We hear of death from air embolus occasionally, probably the correct diagnosis, but the idea that a small bubble of air in a vein is apt to be fatal seems, at best, to be highly exaggerated, as Mark Twain said about the reports of his death.

Our receptionist ushered a Mexican couple into Dr. Thayer's office, stating that the man was needed as an interpreter because the woman spoke no English. After the woman had exchanged her clothes for the usual skimpy examining gown, the husband relayed instructions to her about getting on the table, where Dr. Thayer exposed her chest for evaluation of heart and lungs. Then he propped her up in stirrups for a pelvic exam, explaining each step to the husband and advising him of the findings, which included the discovery of a small ovarian cyst.

As the patient was putting on her clothes, Dr. Thayer addressed the husband: "Your wife may need surgery later on, but there is no great urgency about the operation."

The man showed surprise. "She's not my wife. I just came in to translate for her. I've never seen her before!"

Dr. S. in the nearby town of Kimball shared with me some events that he thought amusing. Many years ago Dr. S. had struggled for weeks to establish a diagnosis on an old woman whose symptoms indicated some obscure form of central nervous system degeneration. The family kept dogging him to come up with a diagnosis, so he finally decided to tell them she had Parkinson's disease, a decision that satisfied the family. They could now tell friends and relatives what she had, although Dr. S. wondered whether he might have done just as well by flipping a coin.

Many years later, the old woman's son developed obscure symptoms suggestive of central nervous system involvement. Unlike his mother, however, he was not content to accept any local doctor's opinion. He insisted on consulting one of the famous large clinics, so Dr. S. happily referred him to perhaps the most prestigious of these, where he was studied and tested in great detail.

After exhausting all the applicable diagnostic procedures, they admitted with some embarrassment that they were unable to come up with a definite diagnosis. "However," they advised, "we are reasonably sure you have Parkinson's disease because we note in your history that your mother had Parkinson's disease."

Twenty-six

Another local doctor became very annoyed with me one day when I laughed at his discomfort. He was just settling himself on the toilet and was unprepared for what would happen when he dropped a cigarette butt into the water. He was not aware that a nurse had dumped waste ether in the stool without flushing it, a fact that was brought abruptly to light with a sudden flashing whoosh that assisted him greatly in standing up. It was, in fact, a very uplifting experience. Also it singed his nether parts. Instead of flush he got flash, and he was not amused when I suggested cheerfully, "It must have been something you et."

The lightninglike quickness of that flash suggests the topic of real lightning. Fortunately, lightning strikes on people are surprisingly infrequent considering the thousands of flashes that occur over relatively short periods. The only such victim ever admitted to our hospital was not badly injured, merely confused from the jolt. What intrigued me about him was the appearance of his skin. He had suffered no severe burns, but on his legs were red fern-leaf patterns of amazing intricacy. Had you dipped real fern leaves, long ones, in red ink, and laid them on his thighs and legs, you would have images of comparable appearance. The images were only first-degree burns. They disappeared in a few days, leaving no mark.

The man had no recollection of having been struck. He remembered only walking across an open field and waking up lying on the ground. The lightning must have struck nearby, as a direct hit would surely have killed him. A neighbor who saw the flash had rushed to his aid and brought him in. The patient apparently suffered no permanent ill effects.

No one knows where lightning will strike. It's what might be called a stroke of fate, like our local Mrs. B's. accidentally killing her chickens instead of her family. As she opened some home-canned beans, she thought she heard a faint hiss of gas. The beans smelled all right, but they had a foamy look that concerned her. Why take a chance? The chickens would enjoy them.

So with caution overcoming her frugal instincts, she discarded the beans, throwing them out into the farmyard to the chickens. Several hours later, she was shocked to find the yard littered with dead chickens. Botulism.

We lost an elderly woman from botulism. She was dying by the time we realized that it was not a stroke. She was part of an unfortunate scenario. She was one of three people who had dined together. Unbeknown to each other, they all became sick, but each consulted a different doctor. All three perished. Had even two of them consulted the same doctor, their condition might have been recognized in time for antitoxin to be flown in from Denver.

House calls formerly were accepted as a routine part of medical practice. The charge in town was three dollars. Country calls were three dollars plus one dollar a mile one way. We felt the mileage fee a bit high since it had been established in the horse-and-buggy days and reflected a time element that had largely been eliminated by fast automobiles. Hence we often charged less.

Fifty years ago, most farms were without electricity, although a few had wind chargers, something that many persons regard as a recent invention. A few others had gasoline-powered generators that supplied a direct current system. I recall only two houses that still had dirt floors, both old stone houses that were surprisingly cozy. The kitchen floors were smooth and so thoroughly compacted with splattered grease that they could be swept vigorously without raising dust.

In contrast to the ultramodern farm home of today, the farmhouse of fifty years ago was primitive. Many rural dwellers considered indoor plumbing a desirable but unnecessary luxury. It took about two years of making house calls for me to remember to approach the patient's bed cautiously so that my size twelve shoes would not give the concealed thunder bucket a hazardous kick. The resulting loud "bong" and possible spill could be embarrassing. I had to think, "Don't kick the bucket."

Since house calls were seldom humorous or amusing, I enjoy recalling one that gave a bit of comic relief. I was summoned late one evening by one of our unmarried schoolteachers. She was in tears when I arrived. Then she laughed, which puzzled me, for she soon resumed crying. In fact, she seemed to be laughing and crying at the same time. Not wishing to waste my time, she tried to establish sufficient composure to describe her problem. "I'd just as well tell you," she began, as she dried her eyes. "I'm afraid I'm pregnant. And after I called you I remembered that you are on the school board!"

In our present "enlightened" age, the situation would not be such a shocker, but forty years ago it was a moral bombshell. And she was one of our better teachers. She was visibly relieved when I assured her that her right of privacy took precedence over my responsibility to the school board, and later we were able to enjoy a good laugh when it was determined that she was not pregnant.

Another call was more urgent. An apartment house dweller got me on the phone: "Come quick, Doc. Mrs. F.'s got her tit caught in the wringer!"

I dropped everything and rushed out to my car, hoping that someone would have sense enough to pop the release on the wringer, yet my concern for her pain was almost overshadowed by the excitement of perhaps having the opportunity to be a witness to this classic wringer accident.

I was too late. The janitor, hearing her frantic screams, had released her. Bust-wise she was very droopy. In fact, her breasts hung down like a pair of socks, and since she was wearing only a loose, thin robe, one side escaped and just naturally got fed into the wringer. That side was pretty well ironed out and quite purple. Luckily, the skin was intact.

A more tragic accident occurred when a young mother was hanging clothes on an outside line. Her curious three-year-old climbed up and activated the wringer, getting a hand caught as it started. His mother was deaf and could not hear his terrified screaming. When she returned to check on him, his arm was jammed up to the shoulder, the wringer still turning and tearing into the flesh. What a heartbreaking situation! The compassion I felt for both mother and child was greatly magnified when I examined the injuries. Muscles were so badly torn that the main artery and much of the brachial plexus (nerve center of the arm) were exposed, necessitating extensive repair.

Thank goodness, he recovered adequate use of the arm, but the poor mother probably will always have frightening nightmares.

Twenty-seven

Hanging up the phone, the nurse exclaimed excitedly, "Your OB is hemorrhaging!"

This highly unwelcome pronouncement was directed at a doctor in a neighboring town, and the nurse was referring to a home delivery the doctor had attended an hour or so previously. "Hemorrhage!" That specter of impending doom that is always waiting in the wings for the chance to upstage success!

Doctor and nurse grabbed appropriate supplies and hastened back to the scene that had quickly shifted from joy to panic.

She was bleeding all right. The pool of blood had reached the edge of the bed and was accumulating on the floor. While the nurse was administering the indicated injections, the doctor was vigorously massaging the uterus and expelling clots from the vaginal canal. Then, leaning closely over the bed, he began packing yards of gauze into the bleeding area. As the last of the packing was tamped firmly into place, he tried to straighten up but felt restricted. The end of his necktie was packed in with the gauze.

Having no desire to disturb the packing, he reached for the nurse's scissors and deftly whacked off the tie, leaving the imprisoned portion as a decorative part of the packing.

When it comes to removing a long, continuous pack of this kind, there is no danger of leaving a portion of it in place. When packing with individual gauze sponges, however, such a mistake can easily be made. A doctor in a town some distance from here committed this error following a delivery, then had the misfortune to be out of town when the trouble came to a head.

Immediately following delivery, the doctor had packed several gauze sponges high in the vaginal vault to retard blood flow that would otherwise swamp the area he was repairing. Suturing completed, he had fished out what he thought were all of the sponges. Two were overlooked. In a week they were offensively ripe, really putrid.

Fearing that she was decomposing internally, the patient consulted another doctor, who removed the stinking sponges—and perhaps sprayed the room with deodorant.

A few days later, her doctor returned. The woman was irate. Confronting him, she raged, "I smelled like a dead rat! I had to consult Dr. K. and *he found two sponges that you had left in me!*"

Her doctor naturally showed great concern. "*He didn't take them out*, did he?" Such savoir faire!

This same doctor pulled a prank on his colleagues. They usually congregated in the doctors' lounge for coffee in the mornings. On this morning our jokester had earlier obtained from Central Supply a clean, new Kotex pad, which he secretly dropped in the large coffee pot. Sipping his cup, he assumed a puzzled expression. "Does this coffee taste funny to you fellows?"

They shook their heads, although one of them reminded him that it was never top grade. "Maybe they used old grounds," Dr. M. mused, lifting the lid and peering suspiciously into the pot. "My Lord, look at this!" he exclaimed in mock horror as he fished the dripping, brown-stained pad out of the pot. "Somebody's got it in for us." Then as he slopped the offensive mass into the wastebasket, one of the more fastidious doctors rushed to the toilet and threw up.

Circumstances sometimes arise when the induction of labor is indicated. Many methods of induction have been suggested and tried, and many have been abandoned, one of which is the use of the Voorees bag. It was a cone-shaped rubber bag and was available in three sizes. Sterilized and empty, it could be inserted with uterine dressing forceps into the uterus, then pumped full of water. Its tube, through which water was introduced, was left projecting from the vaginal opening, where it was clamped off. The bag's inverted cone could now with gentle traction be used as an effective dilating wedge. A stout cord could be attached to a pulley-and-weight hookup if needed, although the mere presence of the bag in the lower uterus would usually suffice to induce labor.

By the time the cervix was sufficiently dilated to let the bag pop out, continuation of labor was usually assured. The bag was especially useful in the uncommon situation when rupture of the membranes failed to induce labor. If the bag were used with membranes intact, it had to be carefully inserted between the membranes and the inner uterine wall.

Two hazards had to be evaluated, the possibility of introducing infection and the chance of tearing loose the edge of a marginal placenta previa when the bag was inflated, should the placenta happen to be attached that low.

I used the bag successfully a good many times years ago and was fortunate enough to escape both of these complications. Now that ultrasound can identify accurately the location of the placental attachment, there might be a spot for the bag's revival, yet for this idea our son the obstetrician shows little enthusiasm.

As a conversation piece, the bag was unexcelled. One concerned husband, a calloused rancher, on observing my cord-pulley-traction arrangement, endeavored to hide his anxiety with a joking comment. He said, "Doc, it looks like you're tryin' to break that child to lead before he can walk."

Twenty-eight

I'd like to mention the Blizzard of '49, how it hampered medical practice and everything else, including life in the country, such as on the ranch where Frank Baumgardner and I were running some cattle and a few sheep a few miles north of Torrington, Wyoming.

It began innocently enough, a few small snowflakes swirling casually in gentle whooshes of breeze. Under a rapidly darkening sky, however, the snowfall and accompanying chilling winds soon gave evidence of what a sailor would call impending heavy weather. Frank knocked snow off his hat as he burst into the kitchen after doing a few outside chores. "She's a bad one," he reported grimly. "You folks had better spend the night. You can bed down on the floor."

He was addressing twenty-two people, neighboring ranch families who were present to celebrate his birthday. Neighboring ranches in this area might be ten or twenty miles away, over questionable roads that can quickly be blocked by drifting snow, and already it was drifting. Snow was being dumped out of the heavens like plastic ghost turds from a huge packing box.

The guests voted to spend the night and make it a gala affair, a real birthday bash. They could make it home next day after the storm had blown out. With that much wind, the storm should be well into Nebraska and Kansas by tomorrow. Yeah?

They were snowbound there for two weeks! Snow piled higher

and higher while the temperature sank lower and lower, staying below zero the whole time. Too cold to snow? Don't you believe it!

Frank butchered a steer and a sheep to feed his guests. Jessie, his wife, had recently brought home a one-hundred-pound sack of flour and twenty-five pounds of sugar, and by raiding her well-stocked shelves of home canning she kept everyone well fed.

In struggling through the sheep shed, Frank became crowded by the sheep against a back wall. The snow, despite being tramped down, had drifted in until the backs of the sheep were brushing the ceiling. Frank was in danger of being crushed, and there seemed no escape. Anxiety must have lent him strength. He was able to pop off a couple of old roof boards and wriggle out through the roof.

Perhaps it was some fortuitous frontiersman's intuition that had prompted Frank to give all the livestock a double ration of feed just before the storm struck, foresight that saved most of them. An animal can survive a terrific storm if it has plenty of fuel in its belly to generate heat. Most of the ranchers in Montana, Wyoming, the Dakotas, and Nebraska were less fortunate. Many lost most of their livestock. Cattle would bunch up in a downwind corner of a pasture and free to death, some still standing up. It was a gruesome time, that Blizzard of '49!

At home in Sidney, I was trying to practice medicine over the telephone. Snow was drifted eight to ten feet deep in many places. Both my cars were stalled, and all roads were blocked with snow.

A frightened young woman called to advise me that she was in labor and that the city weasel (a snow track machine) had broken down and couldn't reach her for the trip to the hospital. Her next-door neighbor was a nurse, whom I then called for help. The nurse could not get her doors open because the drifts were so deep, but she was resourceful enough to crawl out a window and reach the patient. Then I was able to supervise the baby's arrival over the phone. Dramatic incidents were occurring everywhere.

On the fourth day, the snow stopped. People started coming up out of their holes. The huge steam locomotives of the Union Pacific and the Burlington were stalled in the snow. Even their great weight failed to provide enough traction to plow through the deep drifts.

During the early part of the storm, Dr. Shamberg in Kimball responded to an urgent call from out in the country. Wisely he elicited the help of a big country-road snowplow to clear the way. In some flat areas of the prairie the snow had blown almost clear. Wind, of course, moves snow from where you want it to where you don't want it. Thus Dr. S. found that in some places it was easier to leave the road and drive out onto the open prairie sod rather than bucking through snow-filled cuts.

The extent of lowered visibility, even in daylight, can be appreciated when you learn that on one of these detours out onto the open prairie the doctor got ahead of the plow without realizing it. He had a passenger with him, a friend he had brought along in case of trouble. "Step on it, Al," yelled the friend. "We've lost the plow!"

But Dr. S., not wishing to be lost in that vast, unmarked whiteness, stopped the car instead. Just then a fortunate diminishing of the blowing snow enabled the plow driver to see the taillights of Al's car ahead of him. Puzzled, he stopped.

Al's passenger spotted lights behind them and exclaimed, "Some idiot is following us." Then as the plow stopped just behind them, forgetting that the lights on the plow are mounted high up, he shouted, "My God. We're down in a hole. We're gonna get run over!"

After getting squared away and deferring again to the plow's leadership, they were finally successful in locating the right farmhouse. A defective heater had caused most of the family to lose consciousness. "And you know," Dr. S. commented later, "you sure hate to go around opening windows in that kind of weather." Fortunately, no one perished.

On the first day of the blizzard Dr. Bitner was called to the hospital, and since his car was already snowed in he had to go on foot, taking a shortcut across what was then five blocks of open prairie. From Wolf's little home grocery near his home he took a mental heading that should take him to the hospital. He withdrew into the folds of his greatcoat, barely peering out, since there were few obstructions to stumble over. He was buffeted by strong, cold winds that had no constant direction, and he was gaining a new appreciation of the distance across that open area.

Suddenly he bumped into a small signboard. He recalled no such sign near the hospital. Wiping the snow from his eyelids, he read, "Wolf's Home Grocery." Surprise! After all that struggle he was back where he started. He had walked in a circle, and in daylight too, such as it was.

His next attempt was more successful. The hospital was indeed in its usual location, and when he finally burst in through the door in a cloud of blowing snow, he was a welcome figure to both patients and staff. He remained there throughout the storm, aiding the nurses, helping in the kitchen, even giving assistance in the laundry. There was a fireplace in the lobby-reception area, and by keeping a fire blazing cheerfully, Dr. Bitner was able to maintain almost a festive atmosphere throughout the days of imprisonment.

On the day before onset of the storm, we had sent a mother home with her new baby. Over three weeks elapsed before she was able to return for follow-up care, during which time she had experienced a problem with engorgement of her breasts. "The baby wouldn't nurse," she said. "I had to bottle feed him; and my breasts were about to burst. But my dad knew what to do. He put a litter of pups on me, and they took 'em right down!"

Twenty-nine

In 1949 we moved our clinic facilities from downtown to the hospital building to unify our activities and to cut costs. Cash was flowing in the wrong direction. Like the government, the hospital was running in the red every month, the only difference being that here I had to make up the deficit myself. For this privilege I was on call twenty-four hours a day, not only for medical emergencies but for the astonishing variety of mechanical disasters that occur in an older building.

I could not afford to hire someone to do this troubleshooting but soon learned that I could not afford not to. The area that I could *not* relegate was in maintaining staff, and that was the toughest problem, finding and keeping nurses. For what I could pay, few people wanted to come to a small town, although I explained that Sidney had just as romantic a full moon as Denver.

I had four choices: continue subsidizing the hospital, close it completely, raise rates, or get out of town. This last option was perhaps the best. It would eliminate the headache of constantly having to scour the country for help, and I would be relieved of all the responsibilities entailed in running a hospital. But what about the needs of the community?

Perhaps if I were to raise the rates a bit? People were already paying (or at least being charged) $5 per day. Could they pay more? They were paying more in the cities. We would have to jolt the public with a rate increase, go to $7.50 a day, plus a charge for operating room and delivery room and a charge for injectable medications. Until now we had thrown in all medicines.

Furthermore, we would charge obstetric patients a dollar a day for the nursery. This amount did not begin to cover the cost of infant care, but we were dealing with young people who had little money. Even so, this nursery charge aroused some criticism.

One man was irate over our new hospital charges. He had brought his wife to the hospital unconscious from uremic poisoning (kidney failure). Unfortunately, after two days she died, despite special-nurse care at our expense and expensive medication.

When he saw the bill of $62.50 for hospital, doctors, and special nurses, he was so infuriated that he refused to pay a cent. Maybe he was old enough to remember five-cent soup.

A bit later I wrote him a note, asking whether he might feel better knowing that he had paid his wife's final bills himself rather than asking some stranger (me) to do so. He never answered.

Our financial woes were at least partially solved when Marilyn took over as hospital administrator. She had been head nurse for some time and our anesthetist, and she had no desire to be administrator. "I don't want that job," she protested. "I know nothing about it."

"Never mind what you don't know," I answered. "I've watched you work. If there's something you don't know, you darn sure find out how to handle it, and you manage efficiently."

Reluctantly she accepted, and through her excellent management, including further adjustment of charges, she brought us out of the red.

One reason that hospital charges were so low was that all hospital personnel were underpaid. There seemed to be a feeling that one should not expect much financial reward for doing mercy work—a nice Christian thought, but its application failed to put bread on the table.

The advantages of our having consolidated clinic and hospital were demonstrated one morning as we were about to start a hysterectomy. The charge nurse appeared in the doorway of the surgery, hands on hips and with one foot tapping the floor, the very picture of extreme annoyance. "Dr. Cook," she fired at me, "did you tell *five* tonsils to come in this morning? They're not on the surgery schedule."

My heart sank a bit. This had promised to be a very busy day as it was. "I must have," I confessed contritely, "if they're here."

"Well, they're here all right." Then with an amused grin that expressed tolerance of her busy boss's forgetfulness, she added, "We'll manage."

That was Arlene, whose efficiency enabled her to complete a surprising number of tasks while appearing relaxed and leisurely. She knew she would be helping in surgery. By having the clinic in the hospital building I was able to see clinic patients between surgeries, and we were able to finish with the last tonsil by 1:00 P.M.

I'd like to mention an extremely unusual coincidence that occurred in our obstetrics department. A woman was delivered of twins. The first was born at 6:05 and weighed six pounds, five ounces. The second was born at 6:14 and weighed six pounds, fourteen ounces, a combination that will surely not recur any time soon.

One OB was in tears in the early part of her pregnancy after having listened to the ignorant prattling of her neighbors. "Dr. Cook, I'm pregnant again. You know I've had my four C-sections already. What am I going to do?" She had been advised that she had a legal dilemma.

I had missed the significance of her remark and tried to reassure her. "There should be no problem with another C-section."

"But," she wailed, "my neighbors say it's against the law to have more than four C-sections. What can I do?"

"You can tell your neighbors that there is no such ridiculous law. What good would it do to put you in jail? Just relax and quit worrying. We can handle another C-section."

A farm woman consulted me for anginal pain. I explained that her heart was warning her of a possible attack, and I made several suggestions, among them the importance of getting more rest. "Rest!" she exclaimed. "What's that? Everybody depends on me.

It's 'Ma, patch my overalls.' 'Ma, did you feed the pigs?' 'Ma, where's the chain for the tractor?' Ma, this, Ma, that. Why if I was to lie down and die, they'd look down at me surprised like, and say, 'Well, I wonder why Ma didn't get dinner before she died!'"

Late one evening after Dr. Thayer had retired, a worrisome, not very intelligent mother called about her baby, age six months. "Fannie May cain't sleep."

"Does she seem sick or feverish?"

"No."

"Any crying or cough?"

"No. She just cain't sleep."

"Well," explained Dr. Thayer patiently, "it's not necessary that she sleep all night. If she seems comfortable, just leave her alone."

Dr. Thayer was well acquainted with Fannie May's mother, who seemed to enjoy the attention derived from making nuisance calls. He tried to go back to sleep, but an hour later the woman called again with the same complaint. And again Dr. T. tried patient reassurance. Another hour elapsed. Another call, the same whining complaint: "Fannie May ain't sleepin'."

Dr. Thayer never objected to night calls that were legitimate, but this was an unfair intrusion on his brief hours of rest. He asked, "Do you have a bottle of whiskey in the house?"

"Yes," came the rather puzzled reply. "Al's got a bottle."

"OK. Whiskey is a good sedative. Mix a scant teaspoon of whiskey in a little sugar water, and give it to Fannie May. Then *you drink the rest!*"

That woman was not a typical patient. The average person shows remarkable consideration for the doctor's time and schedule. A glaring exception occurred one night after I had retired, when I was called to our emergency room at 11:00 P.M. to see a woman who had injured her back in a fall downstairs.

Fighting off sleep, I rushed to the hospital. The patient looked more comfortable than I as she sat quietly by her husband. Puzzled by this so-called emergency I opened the conversation. "I understand you fell downstairs."

"Yes," she replied. "At the hospital."

"At this hospital?" I asked, feeling more concern.

"No, it was at Roche Hospital," she replied (the other small hospital in town).

I felt annoyed that she hadn't summoned someone over there. "Did it happen this evening?" I asked, trying to disguise my rising indignation.

"No. When was it, Pa?" turning to her husband. "Was it eight years ago or nine?"

This was almost too much. But it got worse. Struggling to uncover a legitimate excuse for her midnight intrusion, I asked, "Is it hurting you a great deal more tonight?"

"Well, no, I guess not. But it's been so long now I figured it was time we done somethin' about it." (But we done nothin' about it until the following day.)

One evening as I was filling my car with gas before making a country call, a smiling young man approached and accosted me cheerfully. My struggle to recognize him must have shown in my expression. "You don't remember me, do you, Doc?" he challenged.

He was right. I did not. Then I remembered a lad we had treated in the hospital for burns. This could be he. "Oh, yes," I bluffed casually. "You got burned."

His laughter was almost a cackle. "By God, Doc, you're right," he answered, gleefully extending his hand in congratulation. Then I did remember him. We had struggled to cure him of gonorrhea.

Knowing my fondness for animals, patients would occasionally bring me orphaned coyotes, skunks, owls, or other critters they encountered on the farm. One night I carried a baby coyote in my shirt front when making rounds at the hospital. There were two children who I knew would be excited to see it. One five-year-old was especially interested. Her eyes widened in surprise and delight when she saw the pup's head protruding from my shirt. Rising up in bed, she announced very firmly, "He *needs* me."

Since the coyote was such a hit with Stacy, I tried the next night with a baby skunk and achieved similar success. The third night

Stacy exclaimed, "What kind of animal have you got tonight?" Sadly I had to confess to an acute paucity of animals. I had planned to bring a young monkey-faced owl, but when it roosted on the hanger rod in my wife's closet, Ruth's patience came to an abrupt end. How do you suppose that owl managed to fly away?

Thirty

From an elderly woman: "My doctor in Colorado said I have gallstones. They're here in my stomach, or in my exhaust pipe. And when they flare up, it excites my piles, and, boy, when my piles get crisscrossed they're really a fright. I need some 'go quick' too while we're at it." Did she mean a tonic or a laxative?

Another woman: "I get such heckalascious headaches. I wonder if some of them transquillers would help."

One of our nurses helped an old woman into the bathroom. A mirror enabled the patient to see herself as she settled on the stool, causing her to become incensed. "Look at that old fool," she exclaimed haughtily, pointing to her own image in the mirror, "watching me go to the bathroom!"

Mood can be very important. A girl complaining of tension explained her feelings: "I've been real nervous lately, and today I'm worse because a guy broke into my house last night."

The incident aroused my sympathy and concern. "Did he hurt you?"

"Not really. I jerked away and ran out the back door. He was gonna rape me, and I wasn't in the mood, so I ran."

After retirement, in doing locum tenens work in other areas I found conditions worse than at home. A young woman with a horribly bruised face explained her appearance: "My husband stomped me. He wanted to rent me out at a dollar a minute, and I wouldn't go for it. So he knocked me down and stomped me." Nice guy. Some people have so little compassion that you wonder whether they deserve to live. This poor woman required careful reconstructive surgery (at taxpayers' expense of course). I wish I could have hired a few thugs to give the husband a good beating. The wife was afraid to bring charges.

We had in our midst a cantankerous elderly man who had made several attempts to bilk insurance companies by staging accidents. His schemes were not clever enough to succeed, hence the hoped-for windfall of dollars never materialized, and since I was the one who exposed him on two occasions I was surprised that he named me as his doctor when he entered a nursing home. For several weeks in the nursing home he hated everyone. Physically, his first problem was constipation. His handling of the problem was, to say the least, unusual. He said, "I get all bound up with chunks I can't pass. I feel like I'm standing on my head because I have to reach up inside and rake 'em out with my toothbrush."

At Christmas the nursing home staff joined with the residents in drawing names for an exchange of presents. Lois, the administrator, drew the name of the toothbrush artist. Later he thought she was the greatest person in the world, but at the Christmas party he still hated everyone. He was downright mean and abusive. Instead of showing some vestige of friendliness when Lois handed him her gift, he seized the package and threw it at her. Then, glaring viciously, he pronounced a dreadful curse upon her: "And I hope you have *a million kids*!" When you think about it, that would indeed be a dreadful curse, all those shoes to buy—and the groceries!

My own eligibility for the "Strange Persons" list might be deduced from the following incident. A bricklayer was working on an addition to our house. I had arrived home for lunch as he was getting ready to start work for the afternoon. He needed some rags, he said, to wipe off the fireplace bricks.

Pondering his request as I removed my jacket, I said quickly, "I certainly can't afford to have you waiting around for rags." And with that I tore out my shirt front and handed it to him. Then I systematically ripped the rest of the shirt to strips and handed them over. He stood goggle-eyed, speechless.

I made no attempt to dilute his amazement with explanations, merely walked out of the room shirtless, leaving him wondering.

What he did not know was that when I had selected the shirt that morning, I had noticed the threadbare collar and had intended to throw it into the rag bag that evening. It was a setup I hated to overlook, and I needed a good laugh. Later I wondered whether I had "smarted out" with that stunt. The bricklayer might question my mental stability and take his family elsewhere for medical care.

But a few months later he appeared as a patient. He had developed a pancreatic cyst that we were able to remove, and during his convalescence his wife laughingly asked about my supply of shirts.

Some nurses use a patronizing editorial "we" in talking to hospitalized patients. One old boy caught a nurse by surprise with his answer. She was saying, "It's our beddy-bye time. Let's go to bed now."

"OK," he shot back, pointing to the bed. "You first."

This man often prayed so loudly at bedtime that he could be heard up and down the hall. I overheard him straining his memory on the Lord's Prayer: "Our Father, who art in Heaven, give us this day our daily bread—Oh, hell! That ain't right." I'm reasonably sure that the Lord's sense of humor would assure the old man's pardon. God must need a good laugh now and then too.

"Doctor, they want you to meet the ambulance at the hospital. It's my neighbor. They're bringing her in. They think she took an overdose of obituaries!"

Now, that sounds serious. Most people can't survive one. I knew she had been somewhat depressed since her father-in-law had moved in with them. Apparently he had been giving her trouble, and I shall spell her complaint the way she had pronounced it: "It's that old man, Doctor; he just hair-asses me and hair-asses me all the time." Sounds uncomfortable, doesn't it? Especially if you're ticklish.

We were successful in pumping the "obituaries" from her stomach, thus eliminating the need for a real obituary.

A mother was concerned about her son following his appendectomy. She advised me, "He ain't urred yet, and his bells ain't moved. I think the nurses are fixin' to give him an enamel." Heady stuff.

This mother was a fine person, honest and hardworking. She just had not been fortunate enough to have had access to education.

I recall a sorrowful woman who was describing what she claimed was constant pain. "Isn't it better part of the time?" I asked hopefully. "No," she wailed, "it's *worse* part of the time!" (So, is the glass half full, or is it half empty?).

A young farmer was brought in with unusual contused lacerations of the scalp. His legs had been pinned under an overturned tractor, preventing his escape. How about the head? That was the interesting part. When the tractor overturned, there had been no injury to his head. But with gasoline running all over his clothes, he became very fearful of fire—so fearful that he sought to knock himself unconscious. A heavy tractor crank lay within reach, and with this he effected the battering I was called upon to repair. He had reasoned that if he were unconscious he would escape the pain of burning to death. His attempts to lose consciousness failed, and as there was no fire and no serious injury to his legs, he was essentially unhurt except for the self-inflicted beating. His "friends" enjoy reminding him of the incident.

We had a quaint little minister as a hospital patient, very pious and serious. It was quite natural that on Sunday morning he should ask the nurse to rummage through a stack of books and periodicals to find his Bible for him. But he soon halted the search. "Never mind, Nurse. If you don't see it, bring me the funnies."

Speaking of ministers brings to mind the girl who complained, "My ministerial cycle is off." She made it sound as if she were going from one preacher to another in some kind of ecumenical routine. Then she added the interesting information, "I cramp hard when I get my ovation." I didn't realize that applause caused such discomfort.

One of the nicest ministers we ever had in Sidney, a fine man in every way, was scheduled for gall bladder surgery. He was fond of our son, whose nickname is Cactus, and he said, "I want Cactus in on this deal. He's in medical school, and it'll do him good to watch you chop up an old codger like me." The "chopping" was successful.

Thirty-one

I was pleased to have on my roster numerous patients from outlying towns. Soon after my arrival in Sidney, I treated a member of a family who lived forty miles away, and it was the noisy appreciation of this family that gave me a following in their area.

The father, age seventy-five, was in extremis from heart failure. He was swollen all over with fluid retention, his lungs were gurgling with moisture, and he was turning a ghastly bluish color. His macabre appearance, depressing in the extreme, had prompted his local doctor to tell the family that nothing more could be done. He was dying. His daughter was reluctant to give up hope. Would I please come and see him?

Realizing that the family wanted at least the satisfaction of knowing that they had done all they could, I agreed to go.

There was no doubt about his being in bad shape. The skin on his legs was splitting from fluid pressure. Heart action was very weak and rapid, as was respiration. Despite such sad condition, his urine showed only a trace of albumen so his kidneys should tolerate a powerful diuretic. I gave him an intravenous shot of salyrgan and told the daughter to be prepared to carry out buckets of urine. Hoping that a lifesaving elimination of fluid would indeed occur, I laid out a few days' medication and departed.

The daughter phoned next day. She was ecstatic. The salyrgan had really worked. Her father was sitting up and eating. A week later, she brought him to Sidney for follow-up. He did not attempt the stairs to our second-story office although he could now walk. I was happy to go down and give him a cursory examination in the car. His improvement was amazing, prompting the daughter to give me a big hug right there on the street.

With his cardiac decompensation now corrected and controlled, he lived comfortably for another three years. And that was how I got a start in that area, by doing a simple procedure which, because of the home doctor's negativism, looked to the family like a miracle.

In good weather a distant house call was no problem except for the way it cut into the schedule. In winter, conditions were a bit tougher. It was Christmas Even in 1937 when a call came in from a farm twenty-five miles out in the country, over in Colorado. A woman was hemorrhaging, apparently from a miscarriage, and "It's snowing too hard to bring her in."

I rushed out there and wound up spending most of the night, while the snow deepened outside. At 4:00 A.M. it seemed safe to leave her. She had apparently passed everything. Outside I encountered a foot of new snow, an annoying complication because it would slow me down, and I had promised my parents that I would spend Christmas Day with them in Boulder, 175 miles away, and Christmas was already four hours old.

In my haste to get back to town, I took a corner too fast and slid into a ditch. The next bit of bad news was the realization that I had loaned my shovel, placing me in a frustrating predicament. Where my car lights illuminated a barbed wire fence I could see a metal sign that recommended chewing tobacco. I tore the sign from the fence to use as a makeshift shovel, but after thirty minutes I was still stuck. I started walking.

Matt Treinen lived only two miles down the road. I headed for his place. Like a dummy, I had rushed out on the call poorly dressed for outdoor exposure. I had expected to bring the woman promptly into the hospital, but she insisted on staying home. Live and learn.

By the time I got to the Treinens', a light showed in their kitchen window—a most welcome sight to me in my half-frozen condition. It was about 6:00 A.M., and in response to my knock I heard an excited child's voice exclaim, "Is that Santa Claus?" I felt like a traitor, arriving as I did without toys or goodies.

When Matt let me in, I was so cold I was afraid I would chill the house rather than having the house warm me. I eagerly accepted his hot coffee even though my teeth were chattering so that I feared I might bite a chip out of the cup.

Matt waited until my arteries thawed, then tossed me a heavy coat and said, "I'll get the tractor." As we rode this tumbling, grumbling beast back to the car, Matt on the tractor seat, with me standing behind, I reflected on Matt's kindness in postponing his chores on this Christmas morning to help so willingly a person who was almost a stranger. I was not even their family doctor.

Yet when I was back on the road ready to roll, the only remuneration he would accept was the return of his own coat, and I realized that any attempt to press money on him would be in bad taste. Thanks Matt.

I was in Boulder by noon.

Another snowstorm experience, also in Colorado, occurred one night west of Peetz, when I drove into a snowdrift. The big caterpillar tractor that had been plowing the road was parked nearby. Quitting time had evidently arrived before the plow had gotten as far as my patient's farm. My attempt to drive past it failed, although after some rocking maneuvers I was able to get free of the snowdrift.

With my car lights trained on the big tractor, I attempted to get its motor started but was unsuccessful. There was nothing to do but wade through deep snow the remaining mile to my destination. This time I was dressed for it.

Another disappointment awaited me. I had supposed that after I had finished caring for the patient someone would drive me back to my car in a truck or tractor. No such luck. The patient's elderly husband was the only other person present, and he looked so frail I was afraid to suggest that he get out in the weather. He might get stuck, and there would be no one to help. I leaned into the wind for the long battle back to my car. Thank goodness for health and vigor.

Many country roads are impassable during and after a bad storm. On a few such occasions I have delivered medicine personally by special delivery air service. After many hours of supervised piloting, I had purchased a secondhand, V-tail Beechcraft Bonanza airplane, a four-place, high-performance craft that soon became a part of the family. Our local airport operators are very efficient at removing snow from the runway. A phone call such as this might come in. "Little Jimmy's got high fever. His throat's awful red, and he's crying with earache. We can't get out. Can you suggest anything?"

"Do you have any ear drops or antibiotics?"

"No. All that stuff got used up."

"I'll see if I can fly some medicine out to you. Tell me exactly where you live." After receiving directions, I might add, "Wave a pair of blue jeans when I fly over so I'll know I have the right place. I'll drop the medicine in a red parachute so you can see it in the snow."

This called for a stop at the drugstore, the fashioning of a parachute from dental floss and a big red bandanna handkerchief, and a dash to the airport. Bonanza 8383-D, my faithful plane, was always eager for flight. Being protectively hangared, it was never buried in snow. A preflight check, a brief warm-up, and we were rolling, a short takeoff roll on these crisp, cold mornings, short because of light load and the increased lift of cold air.

What exhilaration, climbing swiftly into the cold, clear air of a beautiful winter morning! Eluding all the restrictions of ground activity is never routine. In my rising into the sky, all the thousands of years of man's longing to fly have suddenly come to fruition. I'm flying. I check the dials on the instrument panel, those bosom pals that have kept me alive through dark of night and miserable weather.

But today, after the storm, the weather is crystal clear and I can look over hundreds of square miles of snow-covered prairie slipping by at 170 miles an hour while I sit comfortable and seemingly motionless in my heated cockpit, motionless but not unconscious; I'm checking heading, time, and section lines.

That must be the place. He said two metal granaries south of the barn. I buzz the place at high RPM so there will be no doubt of my arrival. Too low for a safe Immelman turn, so I bank and come back for another look. There are the blue jeans all right. A good thing he didn't have to wave the pair he's wearing. I bank for another 180-degree turn and slow down for my bombing run.

Such a blast of cold air with the window open! Out goes the medicine on its cowboy-handkerchief parachute. I waggle my wings and head for home, wishing that there were more drops to make. I never charged for these deliveries. I was having too much fun, and a realistic charge would have seemed exorbitant. Today's fees and costs have me shaking my head. I see in my notes that in 1940 we charged $150 for a gastro-jejunostomy (creating a new opening from the stomach to the small intestine, usually after removal of the lower portion of the stomach because of ulcers and obstructive scarring).

I rarely made actual house calls by airplane and none after an incident that precipitated a jealous reaction. I had made a house call by car, thirty miles out in the country to see some sick children, the Smith family, we'll call them. They had scarlet fever.

Two days later, the father called, suggesting that I come back. I saw little need for wasting his money when my instructions over the phone would take care of the situation. So I talked him out of it, and the kids did recover nicely.

Two weeks later, Smith's neighbor called, asking that I come check his ailing father, a request that came during an interval when I was building up flight time, and since I remembered a level pasture adjacent to this man's house I rolled out the plane and took off. All went well, I thought, until some months later someone told me why I was no longer seeing the Smith family as patients: "Smith is sure mad at you. He says you *refused* to come out to see his sick kids, yet when Old Man T. called, you rushed out to see *him* in your airplane."

One has to save face, of course. I have had more patients leave my roster as a result of my trying to save them money than for any other reason. A frugal attitude is misinterpreted as a lack of interest or a lack of appreciation for the gravity of their illness.

I did use the plane occasionally to transport patients to Denver, or Omaha, or Rochester. And I was once asked to fly a boy from South Dakota to Sidney for surgery. One of the patients I flew to Omaha would have been surprised had he known that I had concealed a heavy wrench at my side with which to hit him in the head should he try to crash the plane. He was being referred to a psychiatric hospital because of two suicide attempts, one of which involved crashing his car. To my relief, he was a model passenger. He took great interest in the flight. The experience actually made him cheerful, causing me to wonder whether flying lessons might benefit him as much as psychiatry.

"Come quick, Doc!" begged a distressed male voice in the middle of the night. "The wife's passed out, and I feel like passing out myself."

"How do I get there?" I asked.

"Go south to Hand's Corner, then east a mile and a half, Then—" a crashing sound as he fainted. I had to have directions, so I waited. In a minute or two he was back on the line. "I guess I passed out."

"We were a mile and a half east of Hand's Corner," I reminded. "Go on."

"Yes, from there you go three miles south and three east—" another crash. Another two-minute wait until he was back on the line.

"Lie down on the floor with the phone," I advised. "Talk lying down." This position enabled him to complete his directions, which must be explicit. Otherwise you can wind up miles from your destination and not know where the error was made. I suggested he open a window. There might be gas in the house.

Speed limits were pretty much disregarded in emergencies, so when I reached what he had described as a three-mile stretch south, I rolled up to seventy miles an hour on the rough dirt road. Imagine my distress when having covered only two of the three miles I came over a slight rise and saw a right-angle turn immediately ahead. I took the turn pretty much sideways, bounced over into an unfenced plowed field, and skidded to a halt, with loose dirt flying clear over the top of the car.

Grateful still to be upright, I coaxed the car back onto the road and continued on course. The couple had not been gassed. They were instead miserably sick with an intestinal infection, probably salmonella. They recovered nicely, a happy outcome. My car fared less well. It suffered a bent front wheel that had to be replaced.

In giving directions, the man had overlooked mention of the fifty-yard jog in the road that had caused my near disaster. This was a "correction jog," an interesting reminder that the earth is round. Lines of latitude are parallel, hence they pose no problem to the surveyor of square plots. Lines of longitude, however, converge at the earth's poles, so if square plots are to be delineated, there has to be an occasional jog in the boundary lines that run north and south to absorb the convergence. I enjoy seeing these reminders that I am living on a big round ball, but I enjoy them more at slower speeds.

The only time I ever drove really fast (120 miles per hour) was in an attempt to reach a suffocated child before it was too late. My only restraint was the realization that I must not wreck on the way.

A two-year-old had been playing on a big pile of wheat in a storage barn. Under the wheat was a chute that opened on a lower level where trucks could be driven in and loaded. After opening the chute on the lower level, the farmer was watching wheat pour rapidly into his truck when suddenly the stream of grain slowed to a trickle, then stopped—a puzzling occurrence because there was still much more wheat on the upper level.

Then he saw it—the little boy's foot sticking out of the short chute, a passage too narrow to accommodate the boy's body.

Never was a pile of wheat scooped away so frantically as on that upper level! But it was too late. The crushing weight of the wheat had been too much. My attempt to intubate the trachea was blocked by a throat full of wheat. I had to cut into his windpipe with a pocket knife to make access for a breathing tube (a catheter). By puffing air into the tube, I was able to inflate his lungs. At sight of the chest moving, the father cried out jubilantly, "He's breathing!"

"No, no," I answered sadly between puffs. "I'm breathing for him. I'm afraid there's no life left." The pressure had stopped his heart. He could not be revived.

Thirty-two

Sometime back there were two sisters in our county who were always trying to out-sick each other. If one suffered from some obscure distress, the other 'ere long was sure to have it worse. This contest went on for years, and it came to an unexpected climax one night when Dr. Bitner responded to their plea for a house call. Sure enough, one of the girls was down in bed and the other was beginning to "feel poorly." But as Dr. Bitner was examining them, they were both badly upstaged by the mother, who lay down in the next room and died! I shouldn't be facetious, but the thought, "How do you top that?" does come to mind. The girls, being very fond of their mother, were shocked out of their symptoms for several months.

A self-styled faith healer summoned me to look at his mother. "There's something wrong with her leg." There was, indeed. When I drew back the bed covers, sight of the leg gave me a shock. From the toes up to mid-calf it was as black as coal, a dry gangrene from loss of circulation.

"I'm afraid we'll have to amputate," I advised gently. "The leg is dead." "Oh, no," replied the son quickly. "We don't want that."

"Wanting or not wanting has nothing to do with it," I explained. "You didn't *want* it to turn black. But it did."

But his mind was made up. There was no use confusing him with facts, and since he also refused any medication to relieve her pain (he wasn't the one hurting), there was no point in my staying with the case. Sometime later I learned that Death had stepped in to relieve the old lady's suffering.

In one country home where I was making a house call I noticed a wide bench in the kitchen. Closer inspection revealed it to be a bathtub cover. The bathtub was in the kitchen to be close to the big kitchen range on which water was heated for baths as well as for cooking. This proximity of stove to tub made for convenient transfer of hot water. The only touch of actual indoor plumbing was the tub's drainpipe that passed through the floor. The source of water was a hand pump connected to a well.

The good people in this house were laughing about an incident that happened a few days previously. The grandfather was taking a bath when a demanding knock sounded on the nearby back door. "Whoever it is," he ordered, "get rid of 'em." Then, because the tub was visible from the doorway, he slid down into the tub, pulling the hinged lid down over him.

A garrulous neighbor woman barged in past inadequate resistance and promptly sat on the "bench," where she prattled on for over half an hour.

By the time she was surreptitiously encouraged to leave, the water-wrinkled patriarch was cold, claustrophobic, and not very tolerant of the family laughter. A good rubdown near the warm kitchen stove restored his comfort but failed to alter his opinion of "gabby females."

Much of the enjoyment and pleasure of dealing with the public has been clouded by the increasing development of the suit-conscious mentality. To us, "suit-conscious" would have meant being aware of what you were wearing. Until recently, we never had to worry about getting signed permits for surgery or other treatment. Our patients realized that their welfare was uppermost in our recommendations. If we said, "Operate," they said, "Go ahead." If we didn't know what to do, we would refer them elsewhere. Such a carefree, trusting relationship did not exist everywhere, but here these people were our friends and neighbors. The suit-conscious mentality has a deplorable effect on all human relations.

I rarely took a nurse along on house calls. In fact, one woman seemed upset when I did. She surprised me by demanding, "Why the nurse? Did you think I was going to attack you?"

"My neighbor thinks he has pneumonia. Can you come out and check him?" This call entailed a twenty-mile drive out into a sparsely settled area of prairie, to an old stone farmhouse that was a bit hard to find because it sat in a low hollow where there were no actual roads, and it could not be seen from more than a few hundred yards away. "You can't miss it." These words are often substituted for adequate directions, as they proved to be here, but a lone horseman who was checking on cattle set me straight.

Although the old house had several rooms, its sole occupant, an aging bachelor, did most of his living in the large kitchen. An antique wood-and-coal kitchen range dominated the room, the only other furniture being the man's cot and a rough table with two chairs. Near the stove were two large fuel boxes, one containing wood and coal, the other filled with sun-dried cow chips. The warmth from the stove offered welcome contrast to the wintry cold outside, but this favorable contrast was offset by the difference in the air. Outside it was clean and refreshing. Inside I was forced to breathe a choking mix of cow-dung smoke, stale tobacco, burned coffee, and body odor.

The patient blended well into this environment. His body and clothes had known each other intimately for some time without interruption. His face, such as showed from under unkempt gray whiskers, bespoke of years spent outdoors. On his head was a greasy black leather cap, apparently for indoor wear since a battered cowboy hat shared a peg on the wall with a tired wool mackinaw, his outdoor outfit. He wore old overalls but no shirt over greasy-looking long underwear.

His age was hard to determine. Being stooped made him look

older, somewhere between seventy and one hundred. But his eyes were clear, and after motioning me to one of the chairs, he sat down on the cot. We regarded each other appraisingly for several moments before he spoke: "I think I got the pneumonia. This morning I hawked up a mouthful of stuff and spit it on the wall to see what it looked like, and where it run down the wall I could see blood in it. Here," he added, "I'll show you."

He followed this promise with a nauseating mixture of coughing and throat scraping until he was able to bring up a dollop of what an old woman I know would call "bloody fleem and corruption."

For some reason, he spared the wall this time. Searching hastily for something on which he could spit and display his prize, he seized one of the bleached-out cow chips, spread the noxious mess generously over it, and thrust it under my startled eyes. "See?" he exclaimed. "Blood!"

Because of this and other findings, I concurred with his diagnosis and recommended hospitalization. But he was adamant on remaining at home. People *died* in hospitals. I did insist on his providing a urine specimen so that I could be sure he was not diabetic. "Do you have a small bottle for a urine container?" I asked. His reply was negative, but I spotted a small medicine bottle on a shelf. "How about that bottle?" I asked.

"Got medicine in it."

"Is it something you're taking?"

"No. But I might need it."

"What's it for?"

"I don't rightly remember. It was for my mother, and she's been dead for sixteen years."

After my persistent, tactful persuasion, he agreed to discard what was left of the medicine so we could use the bottle. I left other medications with him with instructions and departed. I heard later that he had recovered. So had I (from the phleghm and corruption, the ornamented cow chip, and the bad air).

A doctor needs to be very careful in giving advice, as was emphasized to me one day as I was discussing the medication a man had been taking for his "rheumatism." Sometime back a doctor had prescribed a salicylate mixture, and the man had been taking it religiously ever since. "Did the doctor tell you to keep refilling this prescription?" I asked.

"Yes. He said to take it till I didn't need it any longer. I've been taking it every day now for over fifteen years.

I was not surprised that one of his present complaints was ringing in the ears, apparently salicylate-induced.

House calls occasionally uncovered unexpected hazards, as was the case with a certain middle-aged woman who was pretty much an invalid. Her husband was very attentive, but as she gradually became weaker, he was unable to provide the care she needed without quitting his job so he hired a woman to take over when he had to be away. Although not a qualified nurse, this woman had cared for sick people in their homes before and seemed an excellent choice.

After about six months, however, even the woman's excellent care was beginning to prove inadequate. The patient developed sinking spells, when she would be drowsy and very weak, sometimes unconscious. Death appeared to be imminent, although I was able to revive her with stimulants, possibly a questionable act in a case of dreary, prolonged illness.

After several of these crises, I became suspicious. I bluffed the attendant into believing that I had proof that she was trying to kill the patient with overdoses of medicine.

She tearfully confessed that she had come to love the husband. She believed that she could concentrate on winning his affection if the invalid wife could be eliminated. It might have worked.

No criminal charges were filed because I had no actual proof of the "nurse's" evil designs, and she would have denied her confession. The wife, with a different nurse, rallied to live fairly comfortably for another year.

Thirty-three

Dr. Bitner treated a streetwise girl who told him to send the bill to a certain youth rehabilitation center in another state. They wrote back saying that they knew no one of that name, but they thought that one of their charges who used different names might be in our area, and they obligingly sent a picture, asking whether this might be the girl.

I was amused at Dr. Bitner's reply: "My office staff and I feel that the picture is of the girl we treated. However, her hairdo was different, her makeup overdone, and she wore only a brassiere and scanty hip huggers. She had a red heart tattooed on her left buttock and an appropriately pointing arrow just above the symphysis pubis. If this information is helpful in the identification, please transfer our bill to the appropriate account." They paid it.

Problems sometimes arise within families that outsiders find surprising. A young woman of nineteen came in one day obviously disturbed. Reluctantly, she described her problem. "My husband has to be away a lot, and when he's gone my father-in-law comes over for sex. He says it's OK because it's all in the family. But it worries me. It doesn't seem quite right somehow. What do you think? Should I let him do that?"

I pointed out the dangers in such a relationship and advised that family unity definitely need not be carried that far.

This young woman was sweet, meek, and too timid. She needed

more of the aggressive qualities displayed by the bride of a big over-bearing cattle feeder. In explaining her black eye, she said, "He tried to beat me up. So I broke a kitchen chair over his head. He's actin' better now. He's damn near civil."

Dr. Bitner had been with me only a short time when I asked him to respond to a house call from a woman I had seen on previous occasions. My enumeration of her afflictions commanded his attention. I said, "She has heart trouble, high blood pressure, peptic ulcer, nephrosis with partial kidney failure, headaches, and inadequately treated syphilis." Then, as he picked up his bag and headed for the door, I added hastily, "But that's not the problem. She's having an acute asthmatic attack." The asthma he was able to relieve.

When a certain out-of-town doctor brought in a case he wanted to operate on, I asked Dr. Bitner to assist him and keep him out of trouble. I sensed that this outsider lacked the expertise we expected in our operating room. In doing a circumcision on a newborn he had placed so many sutures and ties that the nurse commented, "The poor kid looked like his crown of thorns had slipped down."

In answer to my inquiry as to how the surgery had gone, Dr. Bitner's response was brief, amusing, and disquieting. He said, "You know? Assisting can be exciting."

Perhaps this outside doctor's forte was internal medicine. At any rate, we were soon spared the responsibility of supervising his surgery because he moved to a distant locality.

Other unrelated incidents come to mind. Late one night a very agitated woman called. In the dark she had accidentally taken one of the pills the veterinarian had prescribed for her tomcat. She was greatly concerned that the pills might be harmful to her. "They're to open up his penis so he can urinate better."

Since honest anxiety deserves a courteous answer, I stifled all hilarious witticisms and assured her that she would suffer no ill effects. Laughter had to wait until I had hung up the phone.

One day a small, noisy group came rushing into the hospital in support of a big Swede who had been bitten by a rattlesnake. He was excitedly apprehensive and already beginning to stagger, not from the bite but from the amount of whiskey he had consumed on the way in "to counteract the poison." Over the bite area he was pressing half of a freshly killed chicken "to draw out the poison."

What with all this counteracting and drawing out he should have been in great shape. We had somehow overlooked the value of these measures at the Greene despite that hospital's worldwide reputation for treating snakebite. As we settled him on the edge of the bed, he moaned loudly, "I'm dying!" And he gulped down the last of the whiskey. But as he lay down, he seemed to relax, and he added, "But I don't give a goddamn." He recovered from both bite and booze.

Later that summer I learned another (equally ineffective) method of drawing out the poison when a harvest worker came in holding the base of the snake's severed head or neck over the bite. His friend described the incident: "Damndest thing I ever seen! When Jed reached under the combine for somethin' this rattler bit him on the hand. I thought he was goin' nuts. He grabbed the snake by the neck and bit its head off. Then he jammed the stump on the bite, and said, 'Let's go to town.' He said, 'I've handled snakes all my life, and I'm not about to be done in by this one.'" He wasn't.

When I mention persons or situations that are not medical in nature, it is merely through a desire to display the colorful variety that exists in our community. There was a mortician in town who could be counted on to be eccentric. You might say he was predictably unpredictable. He was having difficulty lining up pallbearers for an old man who had outlived most of his friends. Among several prospects who had declined to serve for one reason or another was one whose excuse for not being able to help was that he had just had all of his teeth extracted.

"Hell!" exclaimed our mortician. "We're gonna *bury* him, not eat him!"

Another local character was dragged unwillingly to church by his wife on an Easter Sunday. Ignoring his questionable eligibility to receive communion, she conducted him to the rail, where he dutifully knelt in quiet conformity with the others, although he felt out of his element. Accepting the wafer, he regarded it with puzzled interest and whispered, "What is it?"

Her reply must have opened his soul to a truly rewarding religious experience. With poorly muffled disgust, she advised, "Just eat the damned stuff and shut up."

Frequently to save time, I would attempt to elicit a patient's history as he or she was disrobing in preparation for examination. Surprisingly, many older people cannot give a history and remove their clothes at the same time. The woman who heads this list in my memory liked to appear on Sundays after church "because we were in town already, and I've had this misery for quite a spell now." With this woman, getting down to the bare facts was time-consuming. Under a heavy coat she wore a sweater, two dresses, one on top of the other, a "gall bladder scarf" wrapped around the upper abdomen, a long-sleeved sweatshirt, and long underwear, and in undressing she would ponder over each garment as though evaluating it for the first time.

I soon learned not to ask any questions while her disrobing was gradually unfolding, for a question would stop all movement in favor of hesitant deliberation. Apparently she could not move and think at the same time.

In direct contrast to this frustrating behavior was that of a young Japanese American woman who came in for examination. I was pleased with her timesaving directness. As soon as the nurse ushered her in through the door, she began describing her symptoms and removing her clothes. By the time she had walked across the room to the examining table, she had already given me half her story and had shed all her clothes. There she stood stark naked, ready for the examination. She was not embarrassed, and there was not a shred of coy sexuality, merely the desire for quick results so that we could both get on to something else. I was grateful.

I rather treasure a remark made by a six-year-old girl who was intently watching me as I wrote a prescription for her mother. I was ordering thirty pills and using the Roman numeral "XXX" for thirty. The youngster regarded the writing with interest. Pointing to the three X's she asked, "Are those kisses?"

"Doctor, a man has just come in with a splinter in his bottom. Can you see him?"

This announcement from our receptionist cut off my already late escape from the office. Of course, I would see an emergency.

As the patient stretched out prone on the table with bared bottom (his, not the table's), I noted an inflamed area that was surrounded by induration, definitely not of recent origin. Near the center of the inflamed area was a small opening that permitted the escape of a few drops of pus. "You think there's a splinter in there?" I asked.

"Yes."

"When did you get it in there?"

"It's been about forty-five years now. It broke off, too deep to get hold of. They told me it would work out. Now this past month I think it's tryin' to get out. It's been gettin' pretty sore."

From his buttock I removed a splinter of wood that was well over two inches in length. This man could not have been a cowboy.

Thirty-four

"I swear on my dead mother's grave, and I've never said that before, that I'm going for the cure." A drug addict was softening up my sympathy before requesting a fix. His memory was bad. He had sworn the same thing to me on two previous occasions.

During my first few months in Sidney, I saw lots of addicts. The reason for their numbers was simple, although it took a while for me to tumble to what was going on. If their condition seemed medically desperate, I would sometimes give them a single dose of narcotic to tide them over until they could get to a larger city. Knowledge of my compassion was obviously passed around the circuit, resulting in my seeing two or three itinerant junkies a week.

I never charged these unfortunates, and if I provided a shot for them I made them take it in my presence so that they could not hand it over to some narcotic agent and say, "Dr. Cook sold me this stuff." Their methods of taking it were ingenious. I'll describe one.

Having just explained to a morphine user that the hypodermic tablets I had would be very unsatisfactory for intravenous use because they also contained atropine, I added, "As many tablets as you need in a shot, the atropine would dry you up so you couldn't spit for a week."

He was undaunted. "I can take it out," he said eagerly.

"How?"

"Just give me four pills, and I'll show you."

Intrigued, I produced four hypodermic tablets containing a mixture of morphine and atropine. "I'll need a blotter," he said. You would be hard-pressed now to find either a hypodermic tablet or a blotter, but in those days of pen and ink, blotting paper was in every office. He placed the tablets on the blotter. Then from within his jacket he brought out a teaspoon in which he boiled water over a flaming match. "Atropine dissolves much faster than morphine," he explained sagely.

With a medicine dropper he carefully dropped two drops of hot water on each tablet. The water passed through the tablets and was at once absorbed by the thirsty blotter. "Now," he continued, "most of the atropine is in the blotter, and most of the morphine is still in the pills which I can now dissolve in the hot water." And he raked them into the teaspoon.

I noticed that the tip of his glass medicine dropper was tightly wrapped with thread to give it the right diameter to fit snugly into his hypodermic needle. While the tablets were dissolving, he used a large pocket handkerchief to tie a tourniquet around his upper arm with a type of bowknot that he controlled with his teeth.

Next he pinched the small bulb on the medicine dropper and sucked up the solution from the teaspoon. By this time, the veins distal to the tourniquet were sufficiently distended to make insertion of the needle fairly easy. He skillfully speared a vein, released the tourniquet with his teeth, and shot the "fix" into the vein. I was impressed. Too bad he did not apply this ingenuity toward some more healthy endeavor.

I remember a woman, aged about thirty-five and rather attractive, who gave me a story that sounded phony, so I checked her arms for needle marks. I found plenty. Realizing I had seen through her story, she became abusively irate but soon aborted her anger in favor of a psychologically different approach: she burst into tears, suddenly a lachrymose object of pity. She said she was sorry she had lied to me. She was on her way to a government hospital for the treatment of addiction, and would I please help her to avoid a collapse before she could reach the hospital.

She wanted "only a small prescription of morphine—even forty grains would help." (That's 160 strong doses for the average man.) This request for forty grains really turned me off. I sent her on her tearful way to try her act somewhere else.

One day our receptionist said she had a young man waiting to speak to me briefly about his wife, for whom he had made an appointment. In came a well-dressed young man who explained apologetically that he would take just a minute. They had just bought the Johnson place north of Sunol—had moved here from eastern Nebraska—and wanted to get lined up with a doctor. He explained that his wife was in the midst of her first pregnancy, that she was badly frightened, and that he had promised to talk to me about being gently supportive. I assured him that I would, and he left.

But in five minutes he was back. "Doctor," he began, showing a touch of embarrassment, "I forgot about my wife's dad. The old man is living with us. He needs medicine for his piles. Here," he added, handing me a slip of paper. "He wrote it down for you. Said it requires a prescription. That's what he uses."

The prescription I was supposed to write got my immediate attention. It waved a red flag. It called for a mixture of laudanum and starch in a cream base, with sufficient laudanum to delight an addict. I looked more appraisingly at the expectant father. He did not show the signs of outdoor labor, nor did he fit the picture of a man who expected to farm the Johnson place.

I advised that if the old man needed something that strong, I would have to examine him. Of course, I never saw any of this fictitious family again, and I resented the wasted time.

Another addict, a colorful character whom I really didn't mind seeing, was a chap whose approach was completely honest. He was considerate enough to say, "Doc, I won't waste your time with some cock-and-bull story. I'm an addict, but I hope you won't throw me out. Perhaps you'll be kind enough to give me enough for one shot so I can be on my way."

I appreciated his directness. He came through about twice a year. In fact, we became friends of a sort. If I had time to visit, he would tell me where he had been, and I would usually provide him with one shot of morphine, gratis, of course.

Once he said to me, "Doc, has a weasely lookin' guy been around here recently for a 'fix,' a guy that uses the name Jacobs, or sometimes Murphy? Have you seen him?"

"He stopped in last week."

"You didn't give him anything, did you, Doc?"

"No. I didn't like his looks."

"For God's sake, don't give him anything. He's a stoolie for the Feds!" I appreciated the warning but felt that I had not been acting illegally. I never charged for a drug given to an addict, never provided more than one dose, and that only if needed for the temporary relief of the severe cramps and other symptoms of deprivation.

Another addict sounded truly serious about wanting to quit drugs. He begged me to put him in my hospital to get him off. "We're not equipped or staffed to handle such cases," I replied. "You would become unmanageable."

"Oh, no! I'll do anything you say."

I had no desire to tackle such a problem in our small private hospital, mine really, since I was owner and operator. Yet he begged so sincerely for help that against whatever better judgment I might have had, I agreed. "However," I warned, "we may have to tie you in bed. And I mean it."

"Fine! OK. Whatever you say."

So with judgment overridden by compassion, I admitted him.

The first day he was cheerful and agreeable, aided by a non-narcotic sedative. The next day he was very nervous and shaky, although still cooperative. He consumed two quarts of ice cream to quell the burning in his stomach. By evening he seemed somewhat confused, insisting on getting up and walking. That was not a problem until he began exploring other patients' rooms, an action we could not tolerate.

"OK," I said firmly, "it's time to tie you in bed."

Evidently he still clung to the idea of cooperation since he submitted meekly to restraint. A straitjacket was not the answer. It would pinion his arms and aggravate his confusion. He should have use of his arms.

I had brought from home my old soft linen climbing rope. With it I encircled his middle, tying him into the central section of the rope and securing the ends to the bed frame, one on either side. Then I crawled under the bed to fashion the final knot where it would be out of his reach. He could now sit up or turn over in bed and was permitted free movement of hands, arms, and legs, but he could not get out of bed.

With this arrangement we got through the next day with only minor problems. During his intermittent lucid intervals, he did not seem displeased with our management.

That night, however, was something else! His screams and yells, punctuated by vile obscenities, were so disturbing to the other patients that I gave up. I phoned the police.

In jail he was only slightly less vocal, but in the morning the police chief reported that our man was quiet and that he wanted to see me. I was quite sure I did not wish to see him. But compassion again prevailed. I went to the jail.

"Thanks for coming, Doc," he said appreciatively. "Can I come back to the hospital?"

"I'd be crazy to take you back," I replied a bit coldly.

"You don't understand, Doc. I don't know what I did at the hospital. Whatever it was, I'm sorry for it; but now I'm OK. It happened early this morning. I was watching some dumb bastard that had his head in the toilet bowl, banging his head up and down like an idiot. All of a sudden I realized that the idiot was me! *I* was banging my head in the toilet! See these lumps on my forehead? From that minute on I've been OK, so can I come back?" I was convinced. He had evidently experienced a real head-to-head confrontation and won. The change was incredible. The police released him into my custody by verbal agreement, and we were on our way back to the hospital.

Had the charge nurse possessed a gun, I'm afraid she might have shot us both when she realized whom I was bringing in. Her quiet stare was venomous. But our man did his best to be a model patient, and after two more days he expressed the desire to be released. "Not fair to you," I advised. "You're not far enough away from the dope."

He continued to badger me, insisting that he was OK. Finally, a few days later I said, "All right. We'll see if you're ready. Here's money to go to the movie downtown. If you're OK, come back afterward and report."

The Snake Pit was playing, a story of alcoholic addiction, and I hoped it might do him some good. He departed, flushed with enthusiasm. "The poor devil," I thought. "That's the last we'll see of him."

But in two hours back he came, cordial and cooperative. "That picture made me think, Doc. Maybe I should stay on a bit."

Two days later, with some misgivings, we sent him on his way, fearing that our efforts had accomplished nothing. In my youthful optimism I had given him a slip of paper on which I had quoted the advice Polonius gave to Laertes in *Hamlet* that included the admonition, "This above all: to thine ownself be true."

"Always carry that with you," I counseled. "Read it often." This action of mine was probably semiromantic drivel. Our course of treatment had been too short for a hard-core addict, and he had admitted to being a longtime user, as was confirmed by the many bluish needle marks on his forearms. These small spot tattoos are bits of carbon from needles that have been sterilized in an open flame.

Three years later, our man was back. I didn't recognize him. He was clean, well dressed, and driving a nice car. He thanked me profusely for getting him off morphine and said he had a good job. He certainly gave every indication of being free of his addiction. I hoped that his gratitude would include an offer to reimburse me for his hospitalization, if not my services. Neither of us mentioned it, however, hence the idea never surfaced.

As we watched his happy departure, I felt glad to have been able to help him. In the same bracket of thought I vowed never again to be dumb enough to attempt rehabilitation of a confirmed addict. It was too difficult in our limited facility.

Thirty-five

In 1954 and 1955 a forward-looking group of local citizens pursued an intensive fund-raising campaign and built a new community hospital, a larger, more elaborate facility than my smaller one. I moved my in-hospital patients to the new establishment, and most of my employees followed.

One of the first obstetric cases in the new hospital involved an infant with a huge oomphalocele, a rare abnormality in which a mass of intestines is herniated out through a dilated umbilicus. Most of the bowels were piled on the front of the abdomen, where they were contained in a thin-walled sac of overstretched peritoneum, the membrane that lines the abdominal cavity. I covered the mass with a sterile gauze pack and called for more instruments.

"What are you going to do?" asked our new anesthetist, a burly, headstrong character who took great stock in her own opinions.

"We're going to put these intestines back where they belong."

"An anesthetic will kill the child!"

"No," I replied, "a few whiffs of ether will suffice. Newborns go under easily. Just fix a sugar tit for diversion. You'll be surprised how well the child will do." I was more concerned with whether the vacant abdomen had grown large enough to accommodate such a mass.

"I'm not giving an anesthetic to a newborn baby," protested the anesthetist loftily, as if she were the only one who appreciated risk.

I found her defiance most annoying. As yet we had not worked together much. I looked at her squarely. "I hope you'll do as I say," I challenged firmly, "because we're going ahead—with or without you." Then, as if she were with us all the way, I added, "Just put that sugar tit in his mouth. You'll find you need only a few drops of ether."

Surprisingly, she obeyed orders, and as things progressed she even became cooperative. Oddly enough, I afterward heard her bragging about our success, emphasizing, of course, that she had given an anesthetic to a newborn. The baby is now a vigorous man in his forties, while the anesthetist has long since passed on to glory. Our problems with anesthetists were not over until Bill and June came aboard. When one of them graced the head of the table, the surgeon could concentrate on the surgery without having to worry about the anesthesia.

Resuscitation of the newborn can be a real challenge. A child that comes out completely limp and the color of raw piecrust may never breathe without help. Vigorous physical maneuvers are definitely not the answer. Intubating the trachea with a small catheter will do the trick if there is still a heartbeat, and do it better than fancy machines.

I recall a large baby who came out looking dead. The child's father, being stable, was allowed in the delivery room, and he watched with moist eyes as I gently puffed air through the catheter. After fifteen minutes the father, struggling to accept defeat, said quietly, "It's no use, Doc. He's dead." Yet I knew something of which the father was not aware. There was still an occasional heartbeat.

In twenty minutes the child gasped, and within an hour he was breathing on his own. He is today a very robust, healthy rancher like his father.

I was grateful when most of our patients readily agreed to hospital deliveries. In home deliveries we encountered many inconveniences, commonest of which in winter was a frigid room. Many early farmhouses depended on a wood or coal stove in the kitchen to heat the whole building. Connecting doors were opened sparingly where heat was needed. In especially cold rooms we could easily see our breath, and the infant, coming out with moist skin, would appear to "steam" as condensing water vapor arose from its body.

A rather exciting C-section (in the hospital of course) was one in which the infant seemed in danger of imminent intrauterine death. At that time, there was no such thing as electronic fetal monitoring. Our monitoring consisted of listening with a stethoscope to evaluate the behavior of the fetal heart as it responded to the stress of uterine contractions. Significant fetal distress then, as now, demanded prompt action.

The woman in question was in her mid-thirties, first baby, and in rapidly deepening trouble. We moved quickly. The anesthetist, in timing the operation, was surprised. "Sixteen minutes to the last suture," she announced loudly, as though we were in a contest. Of course, speed was what saved the baby. It was paramount. Ordinarily, quality of work is more important than speed.

The oldest primipara on our roster was forty-five by the time her baby was born. Since she was past the age of desiring pregnancy, she was furious at the doctor who had told her that because she was entering menopause she could discontinue using contraceptives. It took all the persuasion I could muster to prevent her seeking an abortionist. "At my age," she wailed, "this is ridiculous!" When I finally got her down off the ceiling, she went tearfully on her way, trying to generate an attitude of acceptance.

At age forty-five she had reason to be apprehensive. After she left, I wondered whether I should have been so adamant in insisting that she carry the child. Her age would make her eligible for a variety of complications. What if it should be a Down's syndrome? So she and I both worried throughout the pregnancy.

We need not have. When she arrived at the hospital in labor, she was progressing so well that the possibility of a C-section was dismissed. She had a normal delivery and a healthy baby.

And to my delight and relief, I never saw a prouder, more joyful set of parents. They simply radiated happiness. In fact, it changed their attitude toward life and marriage. Whereas before they had been a somber, colorless couple, they became animated, cheerful, and gregarious. They expanded their circle of friends and started living.

I heard of a shyster doctor who was practicing over eighty years ago who promised his patients their preference, boy or girl, if the expectant mother consulted him early in her pregnancy. His method was simple, ingenious, and dishonest, like the young lady who was purported to be evil, mean, wicked, bad, and nasty—and prosperous.

This doctor kept a book in which he wrote the parents' sex preference. Then at the time of birth, lo, they got what they had ordered. Everyone was amazed and happy. Of course, the system often failed, in which case the parents might be disappointed and angry. In response to their complaint, the doctor would assume an air of the most pious perplexity and say, "Are you sure?"

"Yes, we're sure. We ordered a girl, and this is a boy!"

At this point, the doctor might say, "Well, let's just check back a little. There must be a mistake." He would then produce the book and show it to them. "Right here after your name it says, 'Boy.' See?" And he would be right. What the parents did not know was that he always wrote the wrong sex after their request, knowing that if they got what they wanted they would never ask to see the book.

A few mothers in the delivery room express disappointment if the child is not of the sex they had hoped for. If their disappointment seems acute, it can usually be silenced quickly by asking the question, "Do you want me to put it back?"

Years ago Dr. Cate, a local osteopath who did a bit of obstetrics, sent a messenger to the hospital requesting some umbilical cord tape. He was on a home delivery and was apparently out of cord ties. We kept a supply put up individually in sterile packets. Of course, you can use grocer's twine or any string that's been sterilized, but the tape is less apt to cut into the cord.

I spoke to a nurse. "Give him a packet of tape. No, give him two packets; it might be twins." It was twins.

One young woman was angry because the contraceptive cream we had recommended had failed. Despite using it generously, she had become pregnant. Examination revealed an unsuspected abnormality. She had two of almost everything, except pregnancies. She had a double vagina, the two passages separated by a strong membranous partition, and each passage led up to uterus. With no signs to guide the husband's approach, he had entered the unprotected channel. The pregnancy proceeded normally.

We encountered a more bizarre situation in a primiparous woman (first pregnancy) whose x-rays showed twins, but one was obviously a monstrosity. Our decision to deliver her by C-section proved fortunate. The normal baby was doing well in the uterus, but the "monster" was growing completely outside the uterus, its placenta plastered over the intestines. It was not recognizable as a baby but was rather a sickening collection of imperfect spare parts. Extrauterine pregnancies seldom go to term, and few of them are normal.

Following an obstetrical delivery one evening, Dr. Thayer was recommending to the mother that the baby be circumcised. The grandmother, a loud, brassy woman, would have none of it. She rode roughshod over Dr. Thayer's suggestion, announcing authoritatively, "We don't want that boy circumcised. I've seen the results of an awful lot of poor circumcisions in my day!"

At this outburst, Dr. Thayer merely cocked an eyebrow and murmured a questioning, "Oh?"

Thirty-six

Being a minister's wife must be difficult, especially in the very strict churches, where she comes under constant scrutiny and criticism. It must have been tough on the sparkly bride of a young minister in one of these churches. Her spontaneous ebullience went unappreciated, I fear, in her new role. My office nurse had directed her to step into the dressing room and remove her underpants in preparation for a pelvic examination.

"Panties?" she laughed, lifting her skirt. "I don't wear panties. If you're a good girl you don't need 'em, and if you're a bad girl they just get in the way! I don't wear 'em." Needless to say, none of this conversation ever reached the congregation.

Our people are rugged. We are a community of survivors, a statement I can back with a few examples. A man was driving a big road grader across the railroad track. On his noisy machine, and with his parka hood drawn snugly around his face against the onslaught of winter wind, he failed to hear an approaching high-speed train. The ensuing impact threw him and his machine high in the air, yet he sustained only a couple of broken ribs. His description of the accident was, "I kinda got bucked off."

An absent-minded trucker found himself in the path of an onrushing train. "I couldn't stop, so I tried to gun it across, but the train smacked me good." He required a day in the hospital.

Two elderly women were in a car that was struck by a train. Neither was seriously hurt, although one sailed through the air nearly thirty feet. A young bystander said of her flight, "My math teacher would have said she described a perfect parabola."

A young farmer, an exceedingly brave youth, had an arm torn off by a moving belt. His father in a nearby field could not hear his cries for help above the noise of the tractor he was operating. So the boy kept tossing his severed arm up in the air until he got his father's attention.

The young man survived, and to his credit I must add that I have never known anyone else to make such a cheerful adjustment to the loss of an arm. His fortitude is incredible.

During wheat harvest, a ten-year-old boy who was "riding along" fell off a huge combine (a combination cutting and threshing machine), and before he could get free, a tire of the big machine rolled over his abdomen. The tire was big and soft enough that it distributed the machine's weight over a large enough area that the expected rupture of internal organs did not occur.

Neighbors made accusations to the father the following year after a second accident, jokingly suggesting that he was trying to get rid of the boy. This time the father had run over the boy's *head* with the family Buick. I don't know how it happened. I do know that the boy escaped again almost unhurt because the accident occurred in a very muddy spot. The boy's head was mashed so deeply into the soft mud that it was not crushed.

Patients were always surprising me. This man's voice was urgent. "You've got to give my wife something so she won't feel so good!" Was I hearing correctly? Is feeling good a problem?

"How's that again?"

"I said you've got to give my wife something so she won't have so much pep. She gets all whooped up and goes to town and buys stuff I can't afford. If I don't watch her, she'll snitch several bushels of my corn and sell it in town for spending money. That corn is mortgaged, and if I come up short I'll be in trouble. *We've* got to get her slowed down." His emphasis on "we" indicated that he expected me to come up with a solution.

He apparently did have a problem, but not one to be treated in the manner he suggested. Counseling with this couple revealed that his idea of an adequate female wardrobe was having one dress for "good" and one for work. Surprisingly, both of these people were willing to yield enough that harmony was restored—a fortunate thing, because the wife died suddenly a year later.

Several years farther along, the widower summoned me to his home. He was feeling ill but was not sick enough to be down in bed. When the time came for me to leave, he surprised me by asking if I would like to hear him play the organ. I was amazed. He just did not appear to be the type to be skilled in music. Yet who knows? He piqued my curiosity, and a little relaxation would certainly be welcome.

"Yes," I replied, settling myself comfortably in his easy chair. "I would enjoy hearing you."

With the dignity befitting a true artist, he seated himself on the bench of the old pump organ. His enraptured expression suggested that he must have a deep appreciation of music after all. He sat for a moment, weathered hands poised almost gracefully above the keyboard, apparently waiting for the appropriate aura of inspiration or creativity. The old bellows sighed as they were reluctantly prodded into activity by his manure-encrusted boots.

Then he dropped his hands to the keyboard and began to play. I was hoping for a performance such as was rendered by the man from the creeks in Service's poem "The Shooting of Dan McGrew." Or perhaps something classical to relax by, like Chopin. Not to be!

Under his control, the poor old organ could give forth nothing but discords, no tune, no harmony, merely chance combinations of notes that scarcely knew each other. Wherever his fingers happened to fall, that was it.

I felt embarrassed for him. He had not the vaguest idea of music or harmony. Then I studied his face. He was entranced, like a child with a wonderful noisemaker. He was *playing*. And he was enjoying it soulfully. So what if his "playing" was atrocious? If he was happy doing it, as he obviously was, that was the important thing.

For perhaps five minutes I watched him laying hands on first one area and then another, drinking in the discordant mess like fine wine. I was almost envious of his contented pleasure, and I realized that he was above criticism or sympathy.

I murmured something about never having heard playing like that, thanked him, and started to depart, leaving him to enjoy his happy confusion. He arose triumphantly from the bench, face glowing with pride. "How did you like it?" he asked enthusiastically.

I managed a truthful answer: "I'm really pleased to hear an old pump organ again. I haven't heard one in years."

He seemed to interpret my remark as a compliment. He was beaming with smiles as he opened the door for my escape. Outside, the night was quiet.

Thirty-seven

A surgeon is no superman. Yet to be successful he needs certain characteristics in addition to adequate training. I hate to mention ego. Perhaps I should say "self-confidence." Before he operates, the surgeon must believe that the patient will be better off because of his efforts, and self-confidence has to border on bravado if he is to pick up a knife and start cutting. Here both training and judgment are paramount. Knowing when not to operate is just as important as operating.

In most cases the surgeon has a definite procedure in mind before attempting an operation, but occasionally some unexpected and very alarming condition is uncovered that changes everything. Many times when scrubbing before surgery I have paused briefly to ask the Lord not to desert me in my efforts.

That "simple appendix" may turn out to be cancer of the colon, requiring excision of a section of bowel and subsequent anastamosis (joining together of the cut ends), and the question arises, "How far do I cut? How deep? How much bowel must be removed?" You could teach a high-school student the technique of appendectomy, but he would not have judgment.

Or an artery may slip its clamp and suddenly fill the field with blood, obscuring all visibility, and if it's a large artery, the bleeding can actually be heard. The rhythmic "ch-s-ss, ch-s-ss, ch-s-ss" sound is frightening.

Sooner or later some such unnerving surprise will surface

abruptly; hence to avoid panic it is very desirable that the surgeon be endowed with imperturbable equanimity.

And the surgeon should have compassion—compassion, respect, and gratitude toward those who trust his skill and judgment. Then outside the operating theater, his bravado should yield to humility.

Heavy abdominal surgery under ether before muscle relaxants were available was a challenging experience. Muscles retained much of their resistant tension, rendering exposure difficult, and if during closure the anesthetist happened to ease up on the ether a bit too soon, powerful involuntary spasms of the abdominal muscles would suddenly heave the intestines out onto the front of the abdomen, separating the wound edges and tearing out sutures. And as in Murphy's law, this seemed most apt to occur in obese patients with especially delicate peritoneal tissues that would tear like wet paper. Of course, each tear was at right angles to the incision, requiring additional sutures—more stitches in wet paper.

By this time the assistant, with hands widespread, would be struggling to hold down the bowels under a wet lap pack, at the same time trying to hold the wound edges together. The embarrassed anesthetist would be mumbling apologies through his or her mask and hastening to deepen the anesthesia. Yet even with anesthesia at surgical depth, we never experienced the amazing relaxation of muscles that has now come to be expected routinely through the use of curare-like agents.

When I recall how we had to struggle against muscle tension while doing upper abdominal surgery (gall bladders, subtotal gastrectomies, and the like), it makes me weary. After one of those episodes, when you finally peeled off your gloves, you knew you'd been somewhere. Such recollections remind me that I'm rapidly becoming a "has-been." Most of my contemporaries now have never even seen ether anesthesia. They are part of a new era. More progress has been made in the last fifty years than in the previous ten thousand.

Considerably less than ten thousand years ago we operated on a woman for the removal of a large ovarian tumor. Exploration revealed that it was cancerous and that it had spread into the uterus, the bladder wall, and the lower portion of one ureter. We removed the ovary, the uterus, and the lower section of the affected ureter, and since a severed ureter cannot be left spouting urine we had to do something about that.

It can be tied off—a bad choice, as kidney and ureter will become painfully distended until the kidney ceases to function. The kidney can be removed, more trauma than we wanted. Or the ureter can be grafted into the large bowel, whose function includes the absorption of liquids.

We opted for this grafting. The stools are kept soft, but diarrhea does not usually occur. This woman lived comfortably for another four months before dying of metastases, spreading of the cancer elsewhere.

Perforation of a bowel is not an uncommon condition, and it always demands prompt attention because intestinal matter is leaking, or pouring, into the abdominal cavity, producing peritonitis. It has always amazed me that standing between good health and death from peritonitis is the thin bowel wall, so thin that when it is distended you can see right through it. Often some disease process necessitates the removal of a segment of intestine, a procedure that may be complicated by the need for a colostomy, moving the bowel exit from the anal area to the front of the abdomen. When challenged to accept this different arrangement, many people become depressed.

I attempted to bolster one man's spirits with the following suggestion: "Look at it this way. Suppose everyone were designed with an abdominally located anus such as you now have—where you can see it, reach it easily, and attend to it with both hands. How ragingly irate you might become if some smart surgeon transplanted it to your backside where you had trouble reaching it, and you couldn't even see it without a mirror. Perhaps your colostomy isn't all that bad."

Again I attempted to inject some frivolous, lighthearted cheer into a man who was spinning miserably in the tortured world of vertigo. "It's not a dangerous condition," I commented hopefully. "I've never heard of anyone's dying of dizziness."

I loved his response. "Don't discourage me, Doc. It's only the hope of dyin' that keeps me alive."

Thirty-eight

We were planning a delectable Thanksgiving dinner, a day to remember. Dr. Bitner and wife, Mary, came to help us celebrate. Ruth, my highly capable wife, had labored joyfully to make everything just right and had, as usual, succeeded in preparing a mouthwatering array of goodies. I was proudly carving the turkey when the phone rang.

"Tell them they'll just have to wait an hour," Ruth spoke up apprehensively.

But it was an emergency. A dog, no less, and his intestines were hanging out—just the sort of conversation every hostess hopes for at dinner. The dog had chewed out his stitches following surgery, and the veterinarian was out of town. Could we please do something? "He might try to eat the guts!"

Neither Dr. Bitner nor I can stand to see an animal suffer. We left our disappointed wives, who were trying unsuccessfully to accept this unwelcome interruption graciously.

"We'll have to use ether for an anesthetic," Dr. Bitner stated. "He won't hold still for local."

"We'll need a tin can or a cardboard cylinder for ether," I replied, and as we walked through our kitchen I emptied a Morton's salt container. "This will do to jam over his muzzle."

Dr. Bitner pulled the bottom off the container, and on one open end he fastened several layers of gauze on which to drip ether. Dogs struggle vigorously while going under, but we managed. Then with the dog owner dripping ether we laundered the extruded bowels, rinsing off dirt and debris with warm water. In closing the wound we were careful to place all sutures under the skin where they could not be chewed out.

We returned to a warmed-over dinner and heated wives, but our enthusiastic bragging about our success smoothed the troubled waters so that we still enjoyed a festive dinner, again one to be remembered, although not quite as planned.

Two weeks later, the dog owner came in to pay the bill. The dog was fine. "I don't know what to charge," I ventured hesitantly. "We don't do animal surgery. Just tell the dog to save us a little out of his next paycheck and not tell his friends."

A human counterpart to this incident, at least so far as the evisceration is concerned, occurred while we had offices downtown on the second floor. A young man staggered up the stairs and surprised the people in our reception room. He was trying to hold on to a double handful of intestines, and since the intestines were his own, he had a vested interest in keeping them in place. But they kept spilling out through a big gash in his abdomen and slipping between his fingers.

In answer to the obvious question, he replied, "My father-in-law cut me." (Evidently it was a pretty serious altercation.)

"Why in the world would he cut you?"

"Well," he replied a bit sheepishly, "I 'spect I said something that irritated him." After we captured the bowels in surgery and coaxed them back into their customary confined hideaway, our man readily recovered. Perhaps there is a moral here: "Speak carefully to your father-in-law."

Primitive man got by quite well for thousands of years without circumcision (not the same man, of course). Yet complications can occur, such as in the following case.

"Come take a look at this guy," exhorted Dr. Bitner, catching me in the hallway. "He's got the worst looking penis I've ever seen." And it was the worst I'd ever seen also. The end was ballooned into an inflamed purplish sphere the size of a baseball. Circumcision sixty-five years earlier (or anytime) would have prevented this miserable condition, an infection starting under the foreskin—a foreskin which he said had never been retracted. His glans had never seen the light of day.

He was hospitalized to combat the infection, after which he still needed circumcision, or perhaps I should say plastic surgery. Dr. Bitner had to reconstruct the glans. Its skin had fused with the overlying foreskin, leaving no cleavage plane. It was a challenging mess, requiring sharp dissection and exposing much raw surface.

The next day, finding himself relatively free from pain, the patient wanted to go home, but the raw area was weeping freely and required frequent changes of dressings. The man's wife, a helpless, whining individual, loudly decried any interest in changing the dressings at home. (You met her before: the popcorn lady.)

Up spoke a visitor in the room, wife of the man in the adjacent bed, "I can do that for him. Where do you live?"

This benevolent volunteer had known the patient only twenty-four hours, yet she was offering to assume care of his repulsive member with no concern for the inherent personal man-woman relationship. She saw only another human being in need of assistance. Although not a nurse by certification, her skillful care was an important factor in his very satisfactory convalescence.

One day a teenaged girl was brought in with an obvious "surgical belly," apparently internal bleeding. Operation revealed a ruptured spleen that had to be removed. The people who had brought her in did not know her. Apparently she was a young drifter, walking the railroad track. Luckily for her, these folks had seen her fall as she was walking a rail. When she failed to get up, it seemed obvious that striking the rail had caused some painful injury. Her rescuer's description of what happened next is something of a classic. "We seen her fall acrosst a rail, and wondered why she didn't get up. Then when we seen the train a-comin' we thought we'd oughta run down and pull 'er off the tracks." Good thinking.

We were unable to locate any relatives. Our friendly staff provided the only moral support she received. No one else in the world seemed to care or to appreciate the fact that twice in twenty-four hours her life had been saved by total strangers.

When this unfortunate girl recovered from her surgery, the welfare department took her off our hands, and we lost track of her. The loss of a spleen is usually not a big problem. More tragic was the absence of any family support. She was truly alone.

Such a close call with a train brings up the case of a man I was called to see in a nearby town, a man who had attempted suicide. His horrified landlady had summoned me when she discovered him lying unconscious, surrounded by the most amazing splattering of blood I have ever seen. He had slashed his wrists, evidently believing that such an act would do him in. Of course, it rarely succeeds. Bleeding from small veins stops spontaneously.

Realizing after a time that he was not getting even a glimpse into the hereafter, he slashed his throat, a far more effective maneuver. He had severed his larynx, opened both external jugular veins, and exposed the carotid arteries. Had he opened the carotids, he would have died quickly. Slicing into the jugulars was a bit slower but was about to be just as effective.

With repeated transfusions we were able to revive him. Survival, however, was not in his plan. He was furious. "What right have you," he fumed, "to force me to live?" Then he heaped curses on our heads that might have shattered the morale of a less doughty crew.

We soon referred him to a psychiatric hospital to be purged of suicidal thoughts. As soon as they had brightened his outlook on life, they released him, and it took all of two hours for him to find a railroad track with an approaching train. Waiting until the train was too close to stop, he placed his neck on the rail and offered his head to the iron monster. The train accepted, and this time we were not called upon to waste our best efforts on a failing cause.

I know nothing of the man's background. Perhaps he had never succeeded at anything or realized that the challenges of life supply the zest for living. Life is competitive like a race, and as in a race, the fun of the thing is in the running, not in the finish.

Had we known him much earlier, there might have been a chance of helping him. The psychiatrist got him too late, a sad case.

In contrast to this suicide, I recall a very nice middle-aged man who died very much against his will. On returning on the midnight train from Denver, with no thoughts of death from any cause, he was suddenly stricken with almost unbearable abdominal cramps. After disembarking at Sidney at 2:00 A.M. he became so tortured with pain that he could not stand. No one was about at that hour, no station attendant, no taxi, nobody. So he crawled the seven blocks to his home in utter agony.

His daughter was on the phone at once. Would I please come quickly? Examination revealed unmistakable signs of a perforated bowel. He was moved to the hospital and operated on as an emergency.

Seldom has it been my misfortune to encounter such a mess. The entire small bowel was a mass of perforations through which poured foul, putrid, virulently infectious, irritating slop. Bacteria were destroying the intestine from within and the released enzymes were digesting the intestinal wall from without. The entire gut was being destroyed. Some areas were already gangrenous, a hopeless situation.

After copious saline lavage (flushing) and a quick upper ileostomy, he was closed, with drains everywhere. He died the next day. That was fifty years ago. The massive peritonitis was irreversible, and I see no way we could have saved him, yet the passing of the buck to fate was of little comfort to the family (or to the doctor).

While we are on such an unhappy note, I'll mention a three-pound premature infant who kept turning blue and showing cardiac irregularity whenever his oxygen was turned down a bit. We are not aware in those days of the condition of retro-lental fibroplasia, which is apparently caused or augmented by high concentrations of oxygen given to premature infants. Blindness results. We did not realize that anything as important to life as oxygen could be harmful.

In this preemie's case, however, I am convinced that the child would have died without the high oxygen. So should we save him blind or let him die intact? With modern monitoring capabilities possibly both life and sight could have been preserved, although whenever we turned the oxygen down a bit he became alarmingly cyanotic (blue color from lack of oxygen). I do not know where he is now, but it is my hope that modern eye surgery has enabled him to see.

Another tragedy involved a fat thirteen-year-old girl with a bad appendix. When you're dealing with an only child the risk appears to be influenced by something resembling Murphy's law. Of course, this is superstition, yet it often seems to be operating. Since this girl's parents were visiting a thousand miles away, we had to contact them by telephone to obtain their permission to proceed with surgery.

She died on the table from a sudden cardiac arrest that we could not overcome. Soon after, her father called from somewhere along the road, expecting a favorable report. I had to tell him their only child was dead. At that moment I wished I were a crew member of any low-responsibility job instead of an unsuccessful surgeon who was the bearer of such miserable news. The sadness haunts me still.

Then there was the young man who was told by a navy recruiter that before he could be accepted into the navy he would have to have his varicocele operated on (a tangled mass of veins in the scrotum). He had there the largest mass of varicose veins I had ever seen. The time required to identify which veins should be excised apparently precipitated formation of an intravenous clot that slithered its way up to the heart and into a lung, a pulmonary embolus. It killed him. You can't win them all, but again the losses are burned painfully into your memory, and in these tragic events memory is unforgiving.

Thirty-nine

Some days, such as this one, were more exciting than others. One of our farm women walked in and remarked very casually, "I've been shot." Her tone of voice and level of anxiety were about what you would expect had she said, "I need to go to the grocery store."

Examination revealed not one but two small-caliber bullet wounds in her left arm. Fortunately, the bone was intact. "What in the world happened?" I asked.

"Well, my sister and her husband had a big row. They haven't been getting along lately. This morning she decided to leave and take the baby, but he grabbed the baby and kicked my sister out. She came to our place for help so I went over to see if I could get the baby.

"When my brother-in-law saw me coming up the walk, he came out wavin' a gun and told me to stay away. I said, 'I'm just here to get the baby.'

"'Get out of here or I'll shoot you!' he yelled, and pointed the gun right at me. I didn't pay too much attention to him. I just kept walkin' up toward the porch. He seemed pretty excited and kept yellin', 'I'll shoot! I'll shoot! If you come any closer I'll shoot!'

"But I figured this was no place to leave a baby. So I kept coming, and he kept yellin', and when I got closer, he shot me.

"When I still kept right on coming, he shot me again. I could see the gun aimed at my chest, but he was so shaky he pulled it off center each time and hit my arm. By then I could see that he was serious, so I left."

Her wounds were clean through-and-through bullet holes without arterial or bone damage. They healed readily later on without complications. But as I was completing my initial attention to this brave woman, the sheriff called, requesting my company on a country call where he thought there might be violence. "Some nut," he said, "is holed up in an attic and holding a baby hostage. We may need a doctor, for the baby anyway."

News travels somewhere near the speed of light on country phone lines. When our little entourage arrived, we saw that we were preceded by a group of curious onlookers who were, incidentally, remaining well back from the house. The "nut," of course, was the man who had shot the brave lady.

The man had "forted" himself in the attic with the baby. Obviously, his thoughts of the future did not extend more than a day or two or he would have realized the futility of his position. The appearance of the sheriff meant confrontation, and the sheriff's position was strengthened by the presence of his deputy and a state trooper.

We entered the house without being challenged, but any attempt to ascend the stairs to the attic was greeted with ominous threats. The stairway was very steep and gave access to the attic through a large rectangular hole in the downstairs ceiling. We could talk back and forth with the man but could not convince him to relinquish the baby or to surrender.

While we were distracting him with arguments, the deputy climbed up on a slanting roof outside to reach an attic window. He soon lost interest in the window, however, when a couple of bullets splattered glass fragments in his face.

Meanwhile, the sheriff was formulating a plan of action. He and the trooper were to rush the stairway after firing a cartridge of tear gas. Bill (the sheriff) would grab the baby while Joe covered the attempt with his pistol. "Bill," I advised, "it's too risky. With your eyes full of tear gas you'll have trouble finding the baby. You'll get shot. Let me talk to him."

As yet I had not taken much part in the dialogue with the gun wielder upstairs. Now I hoped, as a doctor, to reach him psychologically. Bill warned, "You're liable to get your head blown off!"

"Well," I replied, "if he won't listen to reason, I'll come back down." Very reluctantly Bill acquiesced, hoping to avoid bloodshed. I called upstairs to the man, "This is Dr. Cook. I'm coming up to talk a bit. We want to avoid trouble. I'm unarmed."

No answer.

I ascended the stairs, saying again, "I'm coming up."

As my head rose above the level of the upstairs floor, I immediately encountered the business end of a pistol barrel barely two feet from my face. The pistol and the man crouching behind it were definitely opposed to my approach. He said, "Stay out of this, Doc. I'm not giving up."

"But you won't be able to care for the baby in this mess."

"That's my business, Doc. Stay out of it! Go back downstairs." I got the feeling he was endeavoring to be courteous, but he was firm. Recalling the bullet holes in his sister-in-law, I reasoned that I had probably trusted my doctor's immunity far enough. I went back down, having accomplished nothing except that I was able to tell Bill the location of the baby.

Both sheriff and trooper were ready for their assault on the attic. Bill fired the tear gas and they rushed up the steep, narrow stairs.

Immediately the "war" started. Seven or eight shots were fired, hence I was immensely relieved to see both Bill and Joe come back down unscathed. And Bill had the baby.

All was quiet upstairs. We waited and waited. Still no sound. Finally, Bill slipped upstairs for a look. There was our man huddled quietly on the floor, dead, shot through the head. "He evidently saved the last bullet for himself," the sheriff concluded. "Looks like he committed suicide."

The trooper concurred, so I signed the death certificate "Suicide" even though when I checked the wound at the mortuary I determined that it had been made by a .38 caliber bullet. The gun barrel that had looked so big when threatening my face was only a .22. The trooper carried the .38. But why tell him he had killed a man? It might have gnawed at his conscience. The days of putting notches on your gun were long gone.

While listing events that happened during my first years in Sidney, I should mention our case of actino-bacillosis, a disease apparently caused by a freakish member of the actinomycetes family of bacteria. I don't even find it in my medical dictionary. The Denver pathologist who examined the tissue samples said there had been only a few cases mentioned in medical journals up to that time (1937). The more familiar form of actinomycetic infection is actinomycosis. Both forms tend to form abscesses throughout the body.

Our victim had been working with cattle, where he may have contracted the infection. His primary site of involvement was the neck, where he had a host of marble-size subcutaneous abscesses. When he refused my urgent recommendations of referral, I summoned an internist from Denver. This consultant probably thought he was being called in to evaluate some run-of-the-mill infection, for when I removed the dressings, exposing the patient's neck, the doctor stopped in his tracks. 'My God!" he exclaimed. "That hits you right between the eyes, doesn't it?"

The neck resembled a sheet of bubble packing material—the kind kids like to step on to pop the bubbles. Only here each bubble was an abscess.

It is possible that the patient suspected he was seeing his last days and that he wanted to spend them at home, for he again refused transfer to Denver even though the specialist explained that his unique diagnosis qualified him for free care as a research project.

With the ineffective medications of that day we were unable to save him. We didn't even have penicillin yet, although I do not know whether it would have been effective. The infection spread downward into the mediastinum, the space between heart and lungs, where a large abscess eventually ruptured, swamping the heart.

We also treated a case of actinomycosis, with equally disappointing results. A woman came in complaining of severe abdominal pain preceded by chills and fever. Examination revealed an intra-abdominal abscess that required operative drainage. After battling several more miserable abscesses and drainages, her exhausted immune system was overcome, and she died. This was in 1941. Modern medication, especially if given early, could probably have prevented her death.

Another unfortunate case at about the same time was a young woman of twenty-three who also required repeated surgery for the drainage of pelvic and abdominal abscesses. We were finally able to get a positive culture and found that we were dealing with tuberculous peritonitis. This, too, we were unable to cure—a most disheartening situation because she suffered for several months. Consultation with the Center for Tuberculosis proved ineffectual. Now we have better drugs.

Forty

I enjoyed orthopedics because of the mechanics involved, getting bones realigned and fragments back in satisfactory position. It is often necessary to improvise to find for each case the solution its uniqueness requires, and I enjoyed the challenge of improvisation.

In 1940 one of our morticians, a large man, fell and broke a hip. He was reluctant to go elsewhere for treatment even though I emphasized the advantages of hip pinning. He preferred to stay home, regarding the hip pinning as a newfangled procedure to be avoided if possible. "Can't you fix it here without surgery?" he asked almost plaintively. "I can try," I answered.

I wanted to save him the discomfort of a hip spica if possible (plaster cast from waist to toes), so I asked his wife to bring in one of his comfortable old shoes, which I screwed solidly to an inch-thick board about sixteen inches in length. With his foot in the shoe we were able to achieve the degree of traction and internal rotation of leg, thigh, and hip that would maintain the necessary approximation of the fragments at the fracture site. This was accomplished by a Rube Goldberg assembly of ropes, pulleys, and weights which I hoped the goddess of healing would, in her benign tolerance, regard favorably.

And she did. He learned to walk without a limp. In retrospect, it looks like dumb luck, although my treatment was in line with what was being done before hip pinning.

Another example of the need for ingenuity arose when we operated on a badly fractured knee in an elderly, obese woman whose x-rays showed a large wedge of bone broken off the tibial plateau (the joint surface of the tibia). I intended placing a long screw through the fragment, hence at surgery I was greatly distressed at finding the wedge itself shattered into innumerable tiny pieces that our x-rays had not delineated. No screw would hold in such a mess.

I called for a sterile rubber mallet, and somewhat to my surprise, I was able to beat the fragments back into shape where they belonged. We smoothed out the tibial joint surface and put on a cast. After a few weeks the cast was removed, and a bit later on she was able to discard her crutches.

Many years later, a visiting orthopedist was pinning a hip in our new hospital, which opened in 1955. Careful following of the procedure by x-ray is essential to assure accurate placement of the metal pin. At a critical point in the operation, a fuse failed. The x-ray machine went dead, and no replacement fuse was available. The surgeon was horrified at being deprived of necessary information in the middle of the operation.

I dropped out of surgery to check on the machine. I noted that the fuse was of the cylindrical type that made contact at both ends. I asked the circulating nurse to see whether anyone in nearby Central Supply had a stick of chewing gum.

"My God, Doctor," expostulated the visiting surgeon in disgust. "You can't fix an x-ray machine with chewing gum!"

I made no reply, hoping that the nurse could come up with a stick of gum that had a metal foil wrapper. She did. I seized the foil eagerly and wrapped it tightly around the fuse, careful that it made contact with both metal ends. Then, popping it into place, I announced (admittedly with a touch of dramatic flair), "Just turn it on." The machine whirred into action.

The surgeon looked at me almost with awe. "Well I'll be damned!" he growled. "There's got to be more to it than chewing gum."

The stunt was no miracle. The only problem with it is that it bypasses the overload protection of the fuse, an objection that can be rectified by varying the amount of foil in the strip, but this is entering the realm of hazardous guesswork.

In coping with any difficult situation I have always preferred the simple solution to the more complicated ones, and in orthopedics there is plenty of opportunity for innovation.

One of my favorite simplifications eliminated an expensive operating room setup, but it was a modality that could be depended on to shock all new assistants. It was my method of drilling a steel pin through a bone for traction. We accomplished the procedure safely in the patient's room without a sterile setup. Any new nurse could be expected to be alarmed almost into inaction at this apparent disregard for sterile technique. "You won't even be wearing gloves?"

"No," I would answer cheerfully. "We're using that old carpenter's drill, and it's not sterile."

"Not sterile?! No sterile drapes? No nothing?"

"The only things that need to be sterile are the skin and the pin and a knifepoint to nick the skin." I would then scrub the appropriate skin area, inject a bit of procaine, attach the unsterile drill pin to the drill, and call for a cotton ball soaked in alcohol, which when ignited burns with a clean blue flame.

Sterilizing the pin (red hot) in the flame takes less than a minute. It can then be plunged into a freshly opened bottle of strong antiseptic solution for cooling, and through a nick in the skin the pin can be safely drilled through the bone. We have never had an infection associated with this procedure.

In other hospitals the patient is wheeled to the operating room, buried in sterile drapes, monitored by an anesthetist, and pored over sagaciously by surgeon and assistant, both conventionally garbed in sterile gowns and gloves. A simple ten-minute procedure is thus colorfully expanded into a production in the mistaken belief that it is all necessary to prevent infection. All it does is add a thousand dollars or so to the patient's bill.

In treating a patient with a broken neck I was preparing to apply Crutchfield tongs to the skull for traction. The tongs sound gruesome, but they are actually much more comfortable than a collar.

They are similar in appearance to the old ice tongs used to pick up blocks of ice, only smaller. A half-inch incision is made in the scalp on either side of the head and carried down to the bony skull, where holes are drilled to accommodate the points of the tongs. These holes do not penetrate clear through the skull, only through the outer table.

A special drill bit is used for making these holes, one that has a collar or stop on it that prevents its going any deeper than three-eithths of an inch. My assistant was a farm girl, familiar with drills and other tools, but she had failed to notice the safety check on the drill bit. She was horrified at the casual vigor with which I cranked the drill, fearing that I would at any moment plunge into the brain and kill the patient. In fact, she was so overcome with sickening apprehension that she fainted and fell to the floor.

Had she been present to observe a certain incident that supposedly occurred during the war in Korea her apprehension would have been justified. I am told of a corpsman who was accustomed to seeing pins drilled through arms and legs for traction. He saw Crutchfield tongs in use in a field hospital, and he assumed that the tongs were attached to a pin that went clear through the head. Accordingly, when he was confronted in the field with a neck injury that needed traction, he confidently drilled a Granberry wire through the head and applied the traction.

The injured soldier miraculously escaped being killed by the procedure, and the first doctor who saw him quickly shipped him to a base hospital. The incredulous doctors there were afraid to disturb the wire. They shipped him stateside at once, where he apparently recovered, fortunate indeed to have survived the drilling, which luckily must have passed through "silent" areas of the brain. If this episode actually happened, one would have to assume that the victim's guardian angel was guiding the wire.

An affable Texan was brought in who had suffered a joltingly painful accident while working on an oil-drilling rig. A thin steel plate had sliced horizontally through his face, shearing off all his upper teeth at the roots and permitting the whole hard palate to drop down on his tongue. With the upper lip severed horizontally at nose level, you could look through the nostrils at the top side of the hard palate and straight on back into the throat.

To effect repair we hooked a wire over the zygomatic arch (cheekbone) on one side and, after raising the roof of the mouth, used the wire to support the hard palate and hold it securely in place. The upper teeth had to be extracted later, testing to some degree the security of our anchoring of the hard palate. Except for the loss of teeth, the results were very good, since the soft tissue repair required only rudimentary plastic surgery of mouth and cheeks.

The patient was so grateful for the success of our efforts that he offered no complaint over having to adjust to upper dentures.

Seldom have I been guilty of tricks in treating patients, yet one busy evening when a very drunk man was brought in with a broken leg, I made an exception. I like to set bones as soon as possible, before excessive swelling renders manipulation more difficult, but this man's behavior made early manipulation impossible. He was about as abusively obnoxious and uncooperative as a person could be. Perhaps a shot of apomorphine would render him less vigorously resistant. Apomorphine has some sedative effect, but I was making use of it here for its function as a powerful emetic, to make him vomit. He was so busy being belligerent that he hardly noticed the shot. I soon began warning him that if he didn't settle down, the reaction from the broken leg would make him sick enough to vomit. "I *never* vomit!" he roared in disgust.

"Well, you will this time," I advised, much to Dr. Bitner's amusement, "unless you calm down and behave."

"Bring that old dishpan," I said to one of the nurses. "He's not cooperating, so I look for him to be sick."

"I tell you I never get sick. Just let me outta here. Gimme back my pants. I'm not gonna—Whoa! Where's that dishpan? By God, I'm gettin' sick!"

After some gut-wrenching vomiting, he was beginning to sober up. He lay back weakly and admitted, "You're right, Doc. Guess I'd better behave." Dr. Bitner was grinning broadly. He knew I had set the guy up, but it was for his own good as well as ours.

An injured older farmer was far more cooperative. No need for tricks here. He had gotten too close to the power takeoff on the tractor. The machine, unforgiving as usual, had snatched out the lower front of his overalls, including one testicle and a portion of the scrotum. Quicker than "scat" he was half castrated.

I was attempting a careful repair under local anesthesia, but he was eager to be up and away. As a senior citizen, he evidently felt he could adjust reasonably well to the loss, for he said almost cheerfully, "You don't have to be so particular with this job, Doc. All I've got left down there is water rights."

One of our farm machinery dealers was another brave man, and just as careless. In demonstrating a new-style combine in a wheat field he kicked a big wad of green wheat down into the hopper—along with his foot. The machine hungrily seized the foot, but couldn't quite swallow it and so ground to a halt.

Since the combine was a new model, no one but the dealer knew the best way to disassemble it. Farmers are good mechanics, but here a different approach was necessary, with special tools. Somehow the dealer kept from fainting while directing his extrication, a process that took nearly an hour. Amputation was unavoidable. The leg was nothing but a messy pulp of macerated flesh and bone, thoroughly mixed with wheat chaff. Amputation a few inches below the knee was our only option. The outward cheerfulness with which the victim accepted his tragic loss made me wonder about a suppressed latent depression, but I never saw signs of it. In fact, he had a good enough sense of humor that he was not offended when I suggested that less heroic measures could be used as a means of getting rid of painful corns.

A man of eighty-five staggered into the clinic in great pain from a strangulated hernia, a condition that demands prompt surgical intervention. Having eaten recently, he was in no shape for a general anesthetic, yet delay might allow time for him to develop a gangrenous loop, greatly increasing the risk, so local anesthesia seemed indicated.

On the operating table he became impatient, and every two or three minutes he would cry out, "Hurry up, Mr. Butcher!" He admitted having no pain from the procedure. The old goat was teasing me.

A chapter could be written describing the various containers people use for bringing in urine specimens. One woman walked a mile carrying her sample in a china teacup. Of course, she wanted the cup back. Our lab technician appreciated this open cup. She had just struggled to shake another specimen out of a narrow-throated perfume bottle whose owner had explained proudly, "I got it in there with a medicine dropper."

The label on the bottle piqued my interest. I wondered whether some daring, adventurous desire had been suppressed here because the woman was the wife of a very somber puritanical minister. The perfume label? "Night in Hongkong."

Another woman, an earthy character who I'll call Wilma Blue, presented her sample in a jelly jar. "I want that jar back," she admonished the technician. "I use it to can jelly."

At Christmas our office nurse gave Dr. Bitner a jar of jelly. She was careful to label it "from Wilma Blue."

A doctor in a neighboring town confessed to me that he had gone to embarrassing lengths to obtain a urine specimen from an intractable old farmer. He said, "I wouldn't do it again," and I could see why when he explained.

He said, "This old boy refused to give me a specimen that I felt was essential. I was about to tell him to go to hell, when his three sons took over the persuasion. With great reluctance the old man finally agreed to void, but only on certain conditions. This momentous event must take place outdoors in the yard. The sons must stand with him in a line of four and all void in unison. Then," continued the doctor, "when I thought everything was all set, the patient balked. 'You too, Doc,' he insisted. By this time I was so caught up in the production that I joined the line. And there we were—the peeing quintet."

Forty-one

I refuse to give a shot to anyone who is struggling so vigorously that I am unable to draw back on the syringe to determine whether the needle tip is in a blood vessel. Injecting vaccine directly into the bloodstream can be dangerous, a fact that was vividly dramatized accidentally on a calf. I was lending Frank a hand at injecting calves to prevent shipping fever and using a metal syringe that made checking for blood impossible.

"This one's a dandy," commented Frank as he held a fine big calf for the shot. In about sixty seconds a helper exclaimed, "What's the matter with that calf?" The unfortunate animal was gasping and wheezing with acute pulmonary edema from anaphylactic shock, a severe allergic reaction. I had, I'm sure, inadvertently squirted the vaccine into a vein. Of course, we had no adrenalin or steroids. We had to watch him die. I felt miserable. I had killed him.

Then I realized the importance of this episode to me. I said soberly, "I'm glad that happened."

Frank was understandably astonished. "Glad?" he blurted out. "Why the hell should you be glad? That was one of our best calves!"

"Because," I explained, "that could have been a child. I'll never again permit myself to give a quick shot to a struggling child without checking for blood to see if I'm in a vein. This calf may have saved some child's life."

I recall one incorrigible kid of ten years who refused to accept an immunization shot. I always felt that it was not my job to force a child to accept shots or treatment. That's the responsibility of the parents. On this occasion, however, events overrode my restraint. The mother was pleading with her son to take the shot. Her lack of control was obvious. He was the boss, she, the subservient lackey whose status was no better than that of a slave—perhaps worse. In his eyes, she existed to satisfy his every demand and to endure his abuse.

To emphasize his defiant dominance, he suddenly kicked his mother viciously on one of her shins. On the verge of tears, she cried out, "Oh, Walter, you hurt Mother!" Then, when she bent forward to rub the injured leg, he landed an upper cut to her face, knocking her off balance.

I was furious. Such disgraceful behavior was not to be tolerated in my office. I grabbed the kid, spun him roughly around, and gave him the paddling of his life, perhaps the only one. (My kids proudly say that on the rare occasions when I paddled them I spanked very hard.) Then I jammed him into a chair and said most firmly, "Around here we treat mothers with respect. We do *not* hit mothers. Now roll up your sleeve!"

He was so astonished that he complied without comment and took the shot without objection. It may have been the first battle he ever lost. He seemed confused by defeat. Many "modern-thinking" people will condemn me for striking this child. My defense is the knowledge that modern permissiveness has filled our jails.

I was thinking, "By spanking this boy I have probably lost this family as patients. If they never punish the kid at home, they doubtless don't want some outsider doing it."

Sure enough, his father was on the phone that evening. But to my surprise, he sounded friendly, said the boy apparently had it coming. He was actually glad that someone had stepped in and taken a stand, something he may have avoided for fear of destroying the love he was hoping to receive from his son. What a tragic mistake. It is difficult for a child to love a parent for whom he has no respect.

Except for temporary superficial resentment, children welcome discipline so long as it is fair. They feel more secure when they know that someone *stronger* than they is in charge, someone on whom they can depend as a pillar of strength in time of stress or danger.

For any doubters I shall make a shocking statement: turning a child into a spoiled, demonic, incorrigible brat can be fatal. His behavior may render examination so difficult that some obscure hazardous condition can be overlooked. Appendicitis can be missed in its earlier stages, and if the appendix ruptures, the increased risk is significant. The same is true of intussusception (where the small intestine becomes inverted within the large one).

But I should emphasize that most children are wonderful. They accept misery and discomfort with surprising equanimity. Kids with fractured femurs tolerate well being trussed up in most unnatural fashion, their buttocks hoisted off the bed in traction that may last for weeks, and they accept this discomfort with hardly a murmur.

Even badly burned kids are often well behaved. Of course, they may do plenty of screaming at the time of the accident, from both pain and fright, but they accept a miserable convalescence better than most adults.

I remember treating little Cindy B. following severe disfiguring burns of the face, neck, and chest from hot grease or boiling water. That child didn't seem to know how to complain.

The same was true of Evelyn A., age five, who came to our office with an itching rash that had raised two-inch blisters all over her body. She staggered in wearing a light gown that stuck to her skin wherever the blisters were breaking. She had to walk with arms extended, legs spraddled out as if she were stradding a stump, yet she neither cried nor complained. I almost cried with sympathy when I saw her. What fortitude! The behavior shown by these kids generated in me a love and respect that I feel to this day.

Any mention of fortitude brings Donna to mind, a twenty-one-year-old having her first baby. She was bleeding. Cautious pelvic examination revealed the cushiony feel of a dreaded placenta previa, a placenta attached so low down that any dilatation of the cervix begins to tear it loose. In this situation mother and baby are usually both doomed to die of hemorrhage, unless C-section is done promptly. So Donna was taken to surgery.

The baby was fine. Donna was weak but essentially all right, at least for three days. Then she became very acutely ill and almost went into shock. Something was terribly wrong, apparently in the abdomen. She showed definite evidence of a perforation. Somehow she tolerated the upright position long enough for an x-ray, and sure enough, under the diaphragm was the slender arc of free gas that clinched the diagnosis of a perforation.

Donna had to be reopened, a frightening prospect in her weakened condition. Yet we had no choice. Operation revealed perforation of the duodenum, apparently what is recognized today as a stress ulcer. Leakage was so widespread that we placed six drains to encourage free escape of irritating exudate, that mixture of pus, serum, and debris that results from peritonitis. To our delight, Donna tolerated this second operation well, but in a couple of days, as we were beginning to lean toward optimistic euphoria, the bomb struck. She abruptly turned blue-gray and went into shock!

If her perforated ulcer was frightening, this new complication was terrifying—a pulmonary embolus! A snakelike clot had broken loose from within a vein in her leg or pelvis and had slithered its way up the vena cava, through the heart, and into a lung. Here was a four-alarm emergency for sure.

Mobilizing all the supportive treatment we could think of, we managed to keep her alive through that most crucial first hour. Then she actually opened her eyes. Now it was hope and pray. In addition to her other problems, there would now be a severe embolic pneumonia.

To combat accumulation of gas, we had passed a nasogastric suction tube and a rectal tube. She was a pitiful sight, having to endure the nasogastric tube in one nostril, and an oxygen tube in the other, plus needles in both arms for blood and other IV support, plus a catheter in the bladder and the six drains in the abdomen. Although it all seemed necessary, I nonetheless experienced acute remorse at having to subject her to such a miserable regimen.

She looked up as I leaned over the bed. "How are you, Donna?" I asked, a ridiculous question under the circumstances. She had as yet not spoken a word since this latest catastrophe.

"Fine!" she replied in a voice that was tiny but resolute. I discovered tears in my eyes. Such fortitude! How could she possibly say, "Fine"? I sat by her bed all that night, hoping that some helpful idea might present itself.

Daylight finally arrived with the encouragement of a bright new day. We were actually winning. And win we did, or rather, *she* did. Donna will always have my highest respect, admiration, and gratitude for her bravery and for her phenomenal defiance of doom.

There was no doubt now about the vision. Father was right.

Forty-two

My easy chair was well named. It had an easy life, for I seldom was permitted the luxury of its consoling embrace. This evening was to be no exception. Before we had finished dinner, the phone rang. Could I return to the office? It was a weak-sounding male voice, explaining that he was unable to pass his urine. "When did you pass it last?" I inquired.

"About four o'clock."

"This morning?"

"No, this afternoon."

"But that's less than three hours. Why the great concern?"

"Because I have an awful lot of pressure. I really need to see you."

It has always been difficult for me to turn my back on anyone who sincerely pleads for help, and this fellow sounded sincere. No doubt he was some old duffer who needed catheterization because of a big prostate.

It was, therefore, a definite surprise to find a man of less than forty years. He looked depressed and uncomfortable. As I was getting him positioned on the table to percuss a probable full bladder, he said something in a low tone that sounded like, "I think I have an apple in my rectum."

Guarding my composure carefully, I tried to recall his exact words. Yes, he had indeed said, "I think I have an apple in my rectum."

"Now *that*," I thought, "is more than a bit unusual." I was careful to show no surprise, since a smirk, or a wisecrack, or even a smile would severely heighten the patient's embarrassment. A good clinician prides himself on being able to hear anything with true savoir-faire. I was thinking fast. It must be a small apple, although larger than a crab apple. That size he could pass.

"Is it a small Jonathan apple?" I inquired casually, in a tone one might use in asking the location of a pain.

The man's hesitant manner disappeared. "No," he stated with more conviction, "I think I have a large Golden Delicious apple in my rectum!"

Well! The cat was now out of the bag. Getting a large Golden Delicious apple out of the rectum would be more of a problem. Using a large speculum, I peered into the rectum. Peering back at me was a large Golden Delicious apple, its original pristine appearance marred by numerous nicks and scratches made by the patient's fingernails.

Here was a challenging situation. Ingenuity was paramount. Perhaps morcellation of the apple would do the trick (cutting it into small pieces), but a few jabs with a Number 11 pointed blade merely pushed the apple higher, rendering it less accessible.

I retired to the back room to search through our collection of obsolete instruments. Possibly something in that assortment of rather frightening discards might be useful. Aha! There was an antique corkscrew curette about an inch in diameter, designed to scrape out deciduous tissue from within the uterus. It resembled a huge old-fashioned gimlet. It might work.

Not wanting the patient to start running off with my speculum, I concealed this gruesome-looking find from his sight. But, alas the curette would not bite deeply into the apple, but merely made it spin in place like a ball bearing.

It was back to the old drawing board—in this case, the antique instrument cupboard. Surely there was something. Yes, indeed! There it was, an old bakelite-handled obstetrics forceps, a pair of tongs large enough to grasp a baby's head. The instrument looked enormous for the search-and-retrieve job I had in mind, and its use would be impossible without first disjoining the blades. Even an individual blade would seem large enough to frighten anyone's anus into rebellious spasm. Yet if somehow such a seemingly impossible insertion could be accomplished, the forceps could then be used to grasp the apple as they had been used to grasp infant heads, and the apple could surely be extracted. But, good heavens! We're thinking of jamming into the rectum an instrument large enough to fit around a baby's head! Clearly some form of anesthesia would be needed.

I picked up the phone. Dr. Bitner was at dinner. "Hmm," he answered with interest. I'll be right down."

"What is it?" demanded his wife, annoyed at the interruption of dinner.

"Hull's got a man down at the office with an apple stuck in the rectum." Mary sat with her mouth open—speechless, possibly the first time he had ever seen her with nothing to say.

He arrived shortly. On seeing the old OB forceps in my hands, his astonishment was obvious. "You'll never get those things in anybody's rectum!"

"Well, I'm going to try. That's why I wanted you here. With a big shot of morphine and just enough ether to approach the excitement stage, it might work."

Then I had another idea. Our patient had gotten the apple in there without benefit of anesthesia and he certainly hadn't swallowed it. Maybe, with enough KY? There are persons who say that given enough of this lubricating gel, it is possible to insert a fence post into the rectum of a gnat.

"Enough KY," I thought. Then to the patient, "I'm going to try something gently that may work. If it hurts too much just tell me, and we'll knock you out."

So saying, I smeared one blade of the forceps with KY and directed it toward the rectum. The blade looked enormous. "It'll never go," Dr. B. commented. And, indeed, he appeared correct.

But after a good deal of gentle wiggling and maneuvering, the blade slipped in and around one side of the apple, with no complaint from the patient. With a gleam in my eye, I reached for the mating blade. At this point Dr. B's pessimism reached a peak. "You'll never get that one in without putting him under." I was inclined to agree. Nobody's anal opening was that big. But being intoxicated with the success I had enjoyed thus far, I forged ahead.

Again careful manipulation paid off. The second blade finally slipped into place. Triumphantly, I locked the blades and prepared to pull. Now, I thought, if only I had the assistance of that student in OB class who pushed too hard on the belly of the mannequin, this cannonball could be fired. Such help proved unnecessary. I advised the patient, or victim, to take a deep breath and push down. He complied beautifully, and as I applied traction on the forceps, there came a sound like a cow pulling her foot out of the mud, and out popped the apple! We were a delighted trio.

We had never seen this patient before. And we never saw him again. In the town not far away where he lived there was a good doctor, but I suspect our man was embarrassed to go to him lest someone in that office leak the story, so eligible for gossip, to the neighborhood. He was so grateful for the subdued, casual manner in which we had handled the problem that he paid double the fee we asked and quickly departed.

Curious as to its exact dimensions, we measured the apple with a tape measure, discovering a circumference of nine and one-half inches. I proudly placed our trophy on a nearby shelf. Next morning it had disappeared. "Edna," I called to the office nurse, "did you eat the apple that was on this shelf?"

"No," she replied. "It looked so beat up that I threw it away."

"That's OK," I said. Then I told her how it had come into my possession. She threw me a murderous glance. "I *might* have eaten it!" Then she looked sick, and I'm afraid my laughter did little to promote good rapport for the rest of the morning.

Forty-three

I'd like to go back briefly to the year 1939, when we admitted a lovable old man who was dumped on us by the county because he was badly in need of hospital care. He was an interesting old Missourian who was in cardiorenal failure, which meant that his heart and kidneys were so swamped with backed-up fluid that they were about to give up. His kidney problems were aggravated by his having an enlarged prostate that prevented voiding. He needed prostatic surgery, of course, if he didn't first die of heart failure or uremic poisoning.

His head looked like a basketball because he was bald, clean-shaven, and his face ballooned with swelling, yet between his slitted lids you could glimpse clear blue eyes that seemed to defy infirmity. He was wheezing and panting as he struggled to help the nurse get him into bed. Yet despite great discomfort he was uncomplaining and cooperative. He murmured, "Thank you, Hon," as the nurse arranged his pillows.

Since Mr. Foster had no money, I was pleased that he was at least appreciative. He expressed gratitude for our care. We accepted all patients at both clinic and hospital regardless of their ability to pay, although indigent cases were an unwelcome drain on our cash flow. The county was supposed to pay for indigents, but the commissioners were often frustratingly penurious, so for several years I had to absorb over half these costs myself.

After several days of catheter drainage and supportive treatment, Mr. Foster seemed sufficiently stabilized for referral to University Hospital for prostatic surgery, or at least he would be by the time he was accepted. After getting his consent, we sent in his application papers.

The reply was not what we expected: "In view of the severe debilitation, the cardiorenal failure, and his advanced age (84), the G.U. department feels that he is not a candidate for surgery."

Now what? Do I tell him he is being abandoned as a hopeless wreck? I went to his room. "Mr. Foster," I began cautiously, "The University Hospital says that their staff is so busy they can't even give you an appointment any time soon."

The disappointment I expected was not there. "That's fine. That's fine," he answered enthusiastically. "I didn't want to go anyway. These little girls treat me fine. They're so nice to me I don't want to leave. *You* can do the operation right here!"

"You know, Mr. Foster, you're not in very good shape. You might not survive the operation."

"I know. But either way, you see, I'll be better off. Either I'll get better or it'll be all over with in a hurry. I'm no good this way, so let's get on with it. You can do it just as well as those fancy doctors in Omaha."

"No, Mr. Foster, I can't. The doctors in Omaha are specialists. They do this operation all the time. I have *never* done it!"

I thought such a confession would smother anyone's enthusiasm. Not so. He said, "You can do it." And repeated, "I'm no good this way. I want you to do it right here."

So after a few more days of preparation, Mr. Foster went bravely to surgery. Of the three possible approaches, the only one we felt we could handle was the suprapubic route, through an incision in the lower abdomen. We lacked the equipment and expertise to do a TUR (a reboring job), and the perineal approach is confusing to a beginner (making incision between the anus and scrotum).

When a prostate enlarges, it bulges up under the floor of the urinary bladder like a doorknob. The bladder must be cut open so that the prostate can be gouged out from its floor from the inside, leaving a raw crater that heals by becoming covered with a growing layer of mucous membrane. Bleeding is a problem but can be controlled with packing, and after it is reduced to a minimum the pack can be removed and the gaping incision in the top of the bladder closed, except for some type of drain.

To flush out clots too large to pass through a catheter, I knocked the bottom out of a glass test tube and sewed the top end into the bladder, bringing the broken end out through the abdominal incision for irrigation. After several days the tube was removed, permitting spontaneous closure of the openings in both bladder and abdominal wall. Mr. Foster was delighted, and so was I. I was also amazed at our success.

After his dismissal, the "little girls" missed the cheerful request he made each night after his evening care: "Blow out the light, Hon."

He lived another ten years before his own inner light was peacefully blown out.

Forty-four

As I approach the time when my own light will inevitably be blown out, I empathize more and more with Mr. Foster, with his character and philosophy. He did not fear death. And since so many people do, I should like to offer some cheerful reassurance by actually putting in a surprising plug for the grim reaper. Death is a comfortable, compassionate escape and rescue from whatever misery may have led up to it. So what is there to fear?

Of course, the question of *when* we die may raise concern because of all the things we would like to accomplish first, but death, itself, is easy.

I am happy and grateful that I was granted the privilege of practicing medicine when doctoring was gratifying and fun. There were few restrictions. We saw what needed to be done, and we did it. Patients were grateful. It was an era that continued to provide ever more effective medications and scientific innovations that enabled us to experience the joy of success where our less fortunate predecessors were often doomed to failure.

As doctors we were there when needed. We never denied our talents, such as they were, to anyone. Thus exhausting demands of giving round-the-clock service were rewarded by the realization that our efforts to relieve pain and suffering were usually successful. I believe that I can stand tall in the knowledge that I never shirked these responsibilities. I feel privileged to have shared Father's vision. It was a good time to be alive.